"Louis Armstrong gave so much
to the world that it'll take them
years and years to realize it."
           Milton "Mezz" Mezzrow

Louis Armstrong

BY HUGUES PANASSIÉ

Photograph Collection by Jack Bradley

Charles Scribner's Sons
New York

This book is dedicated to
Milton "Mezz" Mezzrow,
the best friend of Louis Armstrong.

1 3 5 7 9 11 13 15 17 19 C/P 20 18 16 14 12 10 8 6 4 2

Printed in the United States of America
Library of Congress Catalog Card Number 71-143955
SBN 684-12377-0 (cloth)
SBN 684-13689-9 (paper)

On Sunday, July 4th, 1971, Madeleine Gautier suggested that we call Louis Armstrong on the phone to wish him a Happy Birthday. So we did. In Corona, Lucille answered and said, "Hold on." Then he came on. The voice. Words shining with warmth. Something solemn in the tone, with sparkles of subdued joy. The voice since July 6th, 1971, will remain silent. "Louis Armstrong just went a little further up, he belongs with those rare and blessed human beings whose graves stay empty. Just listen: his heart beats," said a French writer. That profusion of beauty he put in our hearts and souls, all over the world, will stay forever. God bless Louis Armstrong.

Hugues Panassié

CONTENTS

List of Illustrations

Part One
THE MAN

What a warm, good-hearted, down-to-earth gem of a human
being was Louis.

MILTON "MEZZ" MEZZROW, *Really the Blues.*

The New Year was being celebrated in New Orleans. The New Year of 1913. In the colored district around Perdido Street, the crowd waved rattles, blew whistles, and let off firecrackers. Children of all ages were excitedly coming and going; bands perched on wagons blew with all their might at every street corner. A little Negro boy, excited by this uproar, abruptly took leave of his group of friends, shouting to them, "Wait, I'll be back."

He ran toward a house on one of those swarming streets, went inside and came out again almost immediately, flourishing an enormous pistol which he, laughing heartily, aimed at the sky. His friends jumped at the sound of the detonation which made all the passersby turn around, and scatter like sparrows. The small boy, disconcerted by the uproar he had caused, stood rooted to the spot. Passersby who had stopped continued wandering along as though nothing had happened.

A big, tall, white detective came along.

"Was it you who fired?"

"Yes," the child replied in tears.

The detective put his hand on the culprit's shoulder and took him to the Juvenile Court.

"Your name?"

"Louis Armstrong."

"Age?"

"I was born July 4, 1900."

"Your address?"

"Around Liberty and Perdido. . . ."

There was a hearing. The little black boy had taken a .38 pistol that belonged to one of his stepfathers out of his mother's old trunk. No one had been hurt. In spite of the mitigating circumstances, Louis Armstrong, at the age of twelve, was sent to the Waif's Home for Boys, where he had to stay for a year and a half.

Even before this incident, which was to have a remarkable influence on his musical career, Louis Armstrong was interested in everything musical. His ambition then was to sing. In his first book of memoirs* he tells how he and friends would often sing in the evening on the banks of the Mississippi. He had even organized a vocal quartet among the children in his neighborhood and would go singing in the streets or in honky-tonks to earn a few cents. The quartet was called The Singing Fools.

The Waif's Home permitted a small band comprised of the older pupils and directed by one of the supervisors of the home, Mr. Peter Davis. Mr. Davis taught Louis to play the trumpet, or rather the cornet (Louis had already experienced the instrument on occasions when he blew the

*Satchmo: My Life in New Orleans, Prentice-Hall, 1954.

horns of some of the earliest jazz musicians. Louis was gifted with strong lips and vigorous lungs. It was he who now blew calls in the home for waking up, for soup, for baths, etc. In his memoirs Louis says, "I had to blow a call for about everything the boys did. You never saw anything like it—they could hardly make a move without my blowing 'em to it." And he adds, "But it gave me good practice, and I did so well with the bugle that Mr. Davis promoted me to learn the trumpet! And right there my future stretched out shining clear ahead of me, though, of course, I didn't see it then."

Louis became the leader of the small band which played not only for the boarders but also at dances and picnics in New Orleans. Then he returned to his family.

At that time New Orleans was crammed with honky-tonks where black musicians held the limelight. White people went to listen to these small groups, impelled more by curiosity than by enjoyment of the new and spreading music that was jazz. The most popular orchestra was that of a big honky-tonk situated in the Delta district; the leader was the trombonist Kid Ory and the star, Joe "King" Oliver on cornet. As small boys were not admitted, Louis borrowed a pair of long pants from his stepfather and went to listen to the best groups—Freddy Keppard's, The Eagle Band and that of Kid Ory—and not just occasionally, but almost every evening for several years from 1914 to 1917.

One evening King Oliver, who had noticed this young boy's persistent attention, told him to come up to his house to help his wife do errands and shopping for the house, and in exchange he would teach Louis trumpet, or rather cornet—for it was this instrument that black musicians mostly played at that time. The patronage of this famous musician resulted in Louis' playing in several different groups: each time that a musician was unavailable someone would come and get "Little Louie" to play in his place.

Later Louis formed his own band, a very modest one with six musicians: trumpet, trombone, clarinet, guitar, bass, and drums. Joe Lindsay, the drummer, was one of Louis' friends and they decided to appear together in public. Each of these youngsters on his different instrument was directly inspired by his counterpart in Kid Ory's orchestra.

At that time New Orleans was not only well provided with honky-tonks, but music proliferated everywhere. In the streets or in the surrounding countryside it frequently happened that two trucks, each carrying a whole band, would meet and stop. Everyone played in turn, until the crowd and the musicians themselves would elect, by applause and enthusiastic shouts, the victor of this improvised tournament. Louis Armstrong, of course, was already taking part in these musical battles and was already triumphing. Preston Jackson, the trombone player, told of one of these encounters:

> Louis and Kid Rena used to buck every time they met. "To buck" means to try to outplay the other fellow. They were keen rivals. Whenever a dance or a picnic is arranged in New Orleans, a band is hired to advertise on a truck or a wagon. One day Lee Collins was with a band advertising a picnic. Louis was with him, not playing but just riding around. Lee saw Rena coming from the opposite direction in a wagon. Lee was afraid because Henry Rena could outplay him. Louis hid in the bottom of the wagon, so that Henry did not see him. Rena tied his wagon to Lee's so that he couldn't get away. Then Louis Armstrong jumped up and grabbed Lee's horn. The

battle was on and they played until dark. Louis made
Rena give up.

In 1917 Louis Armstrong was offered an unexpected
opportunity. King Oliver decided to go and try his luck in
Chicago, which left his place vacant in Kid Ory's orchestra. Although Louis was only seventeen years old, the
place was offered to him and he accepted enthusiastically.
Farewell to amateur musicians thirteen to fifteen years
old! He was now a professional trumpet player in the very
band which, up to now, he had been able to admire only
from afar.

Kid Ory's orchestra was never idle. Outside of regular
work in the honky-tonks, it was booked for evenings in the
well-to-do sections of New Orleans and its suburbs, for it
was considered the best. Young people from the colleges
also liked to dance to the sound of this orchestra. Louis,
in addition to playing trumpet, did a tap-dance number
as well.

About this time Fletcher Henderson, the leader of one
of the most reputed big bands of the day, wrote to him
from New York, asking him to come and join him there.
Still unsure of himself, Louis discussed this offer with his
friend Zutty Singleton, and it was agreed that if Fletcher
would take Zutty on drums, they both would try their luck
in New York together. So Louis replied to Fletcher in this
way. Alas, Fletcher already had a good drummer. Louis
gave up the venture and it was not until five years later
that he was to accept the invitation, when the famous
band leader renewed it.

One evening while Kid Ory's band was playing on a
truck at the corner of Rampart and Perdido, another
truck came along, also equipped with a band. The battle
began, out of which Kid Ory emerged the victor, thanks

to Louis Armstrong's trumpet. A man at the intersection, watching the scene, asked to speak to Louis. He was Fate Marable, a noted hot pianist and leader of the band on the *Dixie Belle,* one of those excursion steamers which played along the Mississippi between New Orleans and St. Paul, and even beyond that. Such bands, provided to entertain the tourists, were usually composed of white musicians; but, because of the reputation that they had acquired in New Orleans, these profitable posts were beginning to be offered to black musicians. Fate Marable offered to take Louis on in the first black band on the riverboats.

Louis had to think. On the one hand, he regretted leaving Kid Ory to whom he owed his first big chance as a professional musician. On the other hand, he felt a need to get away from New Orleans for personal reasons. Ten months earlier he had married a girl named Daisy, and this union had quickly proved unfortunate. Thinking his absence would allow Daisy to calm down, Louis accepted Fate Marable's proposition and embarked on the *Dixie Belle.* He worked on the riverboats for almost two years. The band consisted of twelve musicians, an impressive number at a time when groups generally had only six or seven members. One of these, David Jones, who played mellophone in Marable's band, gave Louis music lessons.

Baton Rouge, Natchez, Memphis, Cairo. . . . At Cairo, the Ohio enters the Mississippi at the junction of three states, Illinois, Missouri, and Kentucky. After St. Louis and St. Paul came the return to New Orleans. Louis' mother was there to welcome him with open arms. She noted how he had grown. But Daisy wasn't there. Following his mother's advice he ran to Daisy's house; and their everyday life resumed, worse rather than better.

The following summer of 1921 the *Dixie Belle* resumed its course with Fate Marable's band. Louis was more and more master of his technique and from this time played with exceptional assurance in all the registers of his horn. "I had made a special point of the high register," he said, "and was beginning to make my high C notes more and more often. A great strain on the lips. . . ."

A recollection of this period was passed on to us by the white trombone player Jack Teagarden. After telling how (*Esquire*, August, 1944) in 1921 he stayed in New Orleans for two or three days, Teagarden continues:

> In the small hours, a friend and I were wandering around the French quarter, when suddenly I heard a trumpet in the distance. I couldn't see anything but an excursion boat gliding through the mist back to port. Then the tune became more distinct. The boat was still far off. But in the bow I could see a Negro standing in the wind, holding a trumpet high and sending out the most brilliant notes I had ever heard. It was jazz; it was what I had been hoping to hear all through the night. I don't even know whether it was *Tiger Rag* or *Panama*. But it was Louis Armstrong descending from the sky like a god. The ship hugged the bank as if it were driven there by the powerful trumpet beats. I stayed absolutely still, just listening, until the boat dropped anchor. It was Fate Marable's orchestra. Gene Sedric played the saxophone. I talked with the musicians when they landed and Fate Marable presented me to the unknown cornetist with the round open face: Louis Armstrong!

At the beginning of winter 1921–1922, tired of touring, Louis joined Tom Anderson's orchestra in New Orleans and became a member of the brass band called the Tuxedo Band. It was at this time, after four years of marriage, that Daisy and Louis decided to separate.

A few days after his twenty-second birthday in July,

Louis received a telegram from Papa Joe. King Oliver had a place for Louis in his Chicago band and asked him to come and join him immediately.

As soon as he arrived in Chicago, Louis joined the band at the Lincoln Gardens. The group consisted of Baby Dodds on drums, Johnny Dodds on the clarinet, Honoré Dutrey on trombone, Bill Johnson on string bass, and a pianist, replaced a little later by Lilian Hardin, who was to become Louis Armstrong's second wife at the beginning of 1924. John St. Cyr also played banjo in this group, one of the best in the history of jazz. Louis Armstrong took over on second trumpet but seldom played solos—King Oliver would keep all the trumpet solos for himself. But in spite of that Louis was soon noticed by numerous musicians—some of whom predicted that this young man would not be long in eclipsing Oliver himself, who was considered at the time king of the instrument.

In April, 1923, King Oliver's orchestra went on a tour of Illinois, Ohio and Indiana. In Richmond, Indiana, the Gennett Company recorded the orchestra. Those were Louis Armstrong's first records, and he took two solo choruses in one of them, *Chimes Blues*. In his book, *Swing That Music*, Louis says that because of his powerful tone the engineers at Gennett had to place him twenty feet behind the other musicians in order to balance his part with that of the other instrumentalists. Some time after the orchestra's return to Chicago, Lil, finding that Louis was not regularly featured as a soloist in King Oliver's band, persuaded him to join the excellent group of Ollie Powers at Dreamland. Louis had scarcely settled in this orchestra when Fletcher Henderson suggested that he join his band in New York.

Louis accepted and arrived in New York in September, 1924. He saw at last the famous Harlem, about which he had heard so much and which was to American blacks almost what Paris is to the French. To begin with, Louis' appearance was that of a newly arrived provincial. The Harlemites smiled at his clothes and at his big boots. But then they heard him play and it was a different story. He had barely played two or three nights in the Fletcher Henderson orchestra when all of Harlem began to talk about him. The musicians were amazed, stunned with admiration and surprise. It is said that many lost their appetite for several days, the shock was so violent. One thing was certain, and that was that everyone in Harlem was captivated by Louis Armstrong. They watched his slightest movement; they strove to imitate everything he did. The great trumpet player Rex Stewart recaptured in a few striking words the atmosphere that reigned at the time:

> Then Louis Armstrong hit town! I went mad with the rest of the town. I tried to walk like him, talk like him, eat like him, sleep like him. I even bought a pair of big policeman shoes like he used to wear and stood outside his apartment waiting for him to come out so I could look at him. Finally, I got to shake hands and talk with him!*

Among the records that Louis cut with Fletcher Henderson, one created a sensation in Harlem, *Sugar Foot Stomp*, a new title given to the famous *Dipper Mouth Blues* which Louis used to play with King Oliver. Louis had taken the three trumpet choruses by Joe Oliver and interpreted them in a new way.

During his stay in New York Louis also recorded with studio groups, notably that of Clarence Williams with

Metronome, November, 1945

(sometimes) Sidney Bechet on the soprano saxophone. *Everybody Loves My Baby* was such a great success because of Louis' final trumpet chorus that all copies of the record were snapped up as soon as they arrived in the shops, where long lines of purchasers formed. All of Harlem knew this chorus by heart.

After working with Fletcher Henderson's orchestra more than a year, Louis Armstrong again left for Chicago, attracted by a great offer from the director of Dreamland to play in his wife's band, Lil's Dreamland Syncopators. Later, while continuing his nighttime job at Dreamland, Louis joined the pit orchestra led by Erskine Tate at the Vendome Theatre. In addition to jazz, he played arrangements of excerpts from *Cavalleria Rusticana* and other operas. Three of the greatest jazz pianists followed one another into the orchestra while Louis played there: Teddy Weatherford, Earl Hines, and Fats Waller. With Fats, Louis sometimes played trumpet and organ duets.

It was at the Vendome Theatre that Louis made his debut as an actor and soloist. Bill Russell says in *Jazzmen* that at a given moment during the show Louis would climb out of the orchestra pit and onto the stage to interpret his specialty, *Heebie Jeebies,* in such a swinging way that from the very first trumpet notes the public rocked in its seats, shouting and whistling with enthusiasm. Then Louis would sing two choruses, the first one with words and the second without ("scat singing"). He had also recorded the number with the same routine and this scat-chorus became so famous that it was reproduced on the score of *Heebie Jeebies* for both piano and voice.

There Louis Armstrong showed for the first time his gift as a comedian, hardly less surprising than his gift as a musician. He was physically quite small (about 5'4"), broad-shouldered with a short, firm neck, bearing a round, well-shaped head. On his handsome face the most varied expressions followed one another intensely in a sort of rhythm. His alert eyes were constantly in motion. When he played the trumpet and blew hard, his neck would literally swell in such a way as to become nearly as large as his head. His light muscular walk was at the same time lively and sedate, which gave him a free and easy pace on stage as well as on the street, despite the impression created by his powerful, massive back. He would listen very attentively, without seeming to do so, smiling only with his eyes as his mien assumed a surprising gravity. And then, with his head thrown back, staring straight in front of him, his laughter would ring out, sometimes at such unexpected moments that one would look in the direction of his gaze for the cause of his mirth.

In real life, Louis Armstrong is the same as on stage. He is a man who lives every moment with an intensity that is a never-ending show. Whether he is walking along a street, moving around in front of his orchestra, running for a bus, emerging on stage like a star or like a prince; whether he is playing the trumpet with that defiant look of a boxer ready to fight, or meditating on the music he hears coming from his instrument; whether he is telling his friends a story or cracking jokes in a Lenox Avenue bar or in a palace—he gives an impression of strength, of command, of spontaneity, of triumphant power and a love of life wherever it may be. Louis Armstrong's presence in all circumstances radiates dynamic enthusiasm.

During the spring of 1926 Louis left Dreamland to join Carroll Dickerson's orchestra at the Sunset Café, while continuing his work at the Vendome Theatre. At the beginning of 1927 Dickerson left the Sunset and Louis Armstrong became the leader of a remarkable orchestra which included Earl Hines and Buck Washington on piano, Tubby Hall on drums, Peter Briggs on tuba, Honore Dutrey on trombone, Rip Basset, Joe Dixon, Al Washington on saxophones, and Boyd Atkins on banjo. The group was called Louis Armstrong and His Stompers. It was the first orchestra to bear his name and be led by him. But his name had been publicized several months earlier in Carroll Dickerson's orchestra, when bright lights proclaimed "Louis Armstrong, the World's Greatest Trumpet Player."

Records greatly contributed to making Louis Armstrong's name famous. Shortly after his return from New York the Okeh Company had him begin the famous series of recordings by Louis Armstrong's Hot Five, with Johnny Dodds on clarinet, Kid Ory on trombone, John St. Cyr on banjo-guitar and Lil Armstrong at the piano. This small group never existed except on record. The recordings were a wild success with jazz musicians and the black public, *Big Butter and Egg Man* especially becoming the rage.

After leaving the Sunset Café Louis formed a small band including Earl Hines on piano and Zutty on drums (with whom he was to make subsequent recordings for the Okeh label, until he left for New York) but, because of financial difficulties, Louis and Zutty returned, in the spring of 1928, to Carroll Dickerson's orchestra at the Savoy dance hall in Chicago, where Louis again scored an enormous success. At the end of a year the engagement at the Savoy finished, and the musicians decided to leave for New York where the orchestra took the name of Louis Armstrong, who was better known than Carroll Dickerson.

It is impossible to give an idea of Louis Armstrong's success and the scope of his influence upon all Chicago musicians during those years. At the Sunset and Savoy people swarmed to hear him. Not only the black musicians but also the best white Chicago musicians crowded around him and rushed to listen to him as soon as their own jobs were finished. Bix Beiderbecke said, "No musician exists beside Louis Armstrong." The group known as the Chicagoans and comprised of Mezz Mezzrow, Muggsy Spanier, Jess Stacy, George Wettling, Frank Teschemacher, Dave Tough, Gene Krupa, and Bud Freeman, was not satisfied to just listen to Louis. During intermissions Muggsy replaced him on the trumpet, while Jess Stacy took over from Earl Hines at the piano; others did the same and these white musicians endeavored to make the same music as their black idols. Sometimes jam sessions took place in which everyone played together. One night Muggsy, being particularly inspired, improvised such fine choruses that Earl Hines came to Louis Armstrong and teased him, saying, "This time he's got you!" But Louis took up his trumpet again and completely outblew Muggsy.

These battles among musicians playing the same instrument were not rare. Sometimes an indiscreet trumpet player tried his hand at playing before or after Louis to outdo him; he never tried again. When Louis Armstrong's merit was universally recognized, no instrumentalist dared challenge him. Previously, many of the famous trumpet players who had underestimated Louis, or who were overconfident, had discomfiting experiences. For instance, at the end of 1925 when Louis was playing at Dreamland in his wife's orchestra, one of the best trumpet players in New Orleans of King Oliver's generation, Freddie Keppard, came into the night club and said to Louis, "Give me your trumpet a minute." Keppard began to play and when the demonstration was finished gave the trumpet back to Louis with a careless and haughty gesture. "Take care of him, Louis, take care of him!" the other musicians shouted. Louis took such good care of him that when he finished playing the club roared with enthusiasm—and Keppard had disappeared.

Although he was loaded with work—recordings in the morning, afternoon and evening, engagements at the Vendome Theatre, and afterward at the Sunset—Louis Armstrong had such endurance and loved playing so much that when his work at the Sunset was finished he would go to other clubs with a group of musicians and play for hours, improvising ten, fifteen, twenty choruses in a row, surrounded by enthusiasts shouting with joy or crying with emotion. Some, after hearing Louis play, could not or did not want to speak for several days—the experience had been so moving. Louis did not go to bed until late each morning, if he had time, which was not always the case. But fatigue did not seem to distress him, and photographs of this period show him overflowing with health and extremely stout.

In New York after some difficulty the orchestra was signed on at the Savoy, the big dance hall in Harlem, then at Connie's Inn, to accompany the famous *Hot Chocolates* show whose music was partly composed by Fats Waller. It was then that *Ain't Misbehavin'* was released, the famous number that Louis Armstrong interpreted on stage, scoring a new triumph every evening. When he had finished playing the first night, all the musicians accompanying the show spontaneously arose from the pit to add their applause to that of the audience.

After staying at Connie's Inn from the fall of 1929 to the spring of 1930, Louis Armstrong took over the leadership of the Luis Russell orchestra and went on tour in various parts of the United States. From that time on Louis frequently changed orchestras, usually putting himself at the head of already existing groups, momentarily becoming their leader. After leaving Luis Russell's band in 1930, he was accompanied by the Cocoanut Grove orchestra, which the following year formed the nucleus of the famous Blue Rhythm Band. Toward the end of 1930, he led a small orchestra in Hollywood at Sebastian's Cotton Club. Among its members were Lawrence Brown on trombone and Lionel Hampton on drums. Next he led the California orchestra of Les Hite, still including Hampton but without Lawrence Brown. It was during this stay in Hollywood that Louis made his first film, an animated sketch where his head was seen in close-up, singing *You Rascal You* in a menacing but humorous way.

Back in Chicago, around the spring of 1931, Louis assembled nine musicians from the town and formed an orchestra which, this time, was really his own; it included Tubby Hall on drums and John Lindsay on string bass. With this group he returned to his home town for the first time, and in June, 1931, the black population of New Orleans gave their famous compatriot a triumphant reception. From there Louis returned again to New York to play at the Lafayette Theatre. Then he gave up his orchestra and returned to California, where he resumed work with the Les Hite group. It was from there that he decided, in 1932, to go to Europe. Accompanied by his manager, Johnny Collins, he arrived in England in July, aboard the S.S. *Majestic.*

Louis Armstrong was quite surprised to discover how well known he was in Europe. He had not realized how famous his records had become all over the world. As soon as he arrived he was made guest of honor at a banquet of press representatives and jazz orchestra leaders. He was described by the journalists as "a small, slim man carrying an enormous white cap and a long putty-colored overcoat"—for Louis had lost weight during the preceding years and scarcely resembled his old photographs.

Louis played at the Palladium for a fortnight, accompanied by black musicians who had come from Paris. His success was vast and with them he toured England and Scotland. When the musicians from his orchestra had to go back to Paris he changed groups and was accompanied by English musicians.

Paris received a visit from Louis Armstrong the following October, but his manager made such exorbitant financial demands that no booking could be effected. Louis left Paris after a few days without having made himself heard in France.

Returning to New York at the beginning of November, Louis put himself at the head of Chick Webb's orchestra. At that time his lips caused him pain. On several occasions, the state of his lips gave place to dramatic scenes. Mezz Mezzrow says in his book, *Really the Blues,* that Louis' lip was so bad that "it looked like he had a big overgrown strawberry setting on it." One evening in Baltimore, while Louis played *Them There Eyes* with superhuman effort, his lips split. Each note he then played was agony. Musicians and chorus girls, their eyes fixed on him, could not conceal their emotion. Suddenly they saw Charlie Green, the trombonist, leave the stage and burst into tears. Louis had to finish with a high F. Chick Webb, also in tears, "used all the masterful techniques he knew on the drums" to help him. With his face bleeding and perspiring, "Louis clutched and crawled and made that high F on his hands and knees." A thunder of applause rose from the hall while Louis "managed to smile and bow and smile again, making pretty for the people."

Louis returned to Chicago, his home port, at the beginning of 1933. One of his letters, published by the

English review *The Melody Maker*—the first text of Louis Armstrong's to appear in print—mentions this return:

> I am now at home, in Chicago, and enjoying myself to the highest. The first thing I had for supper the first day I arrived in the ol' home town was a big pot of good red beans and rice, ha, ha, ha. . . . I had to pull myself up from the table, ha, ha. . . . And then I went and heard Ol' Father Hines get off for me last night. And boy did he play that piano? He made that piano say "Goodness gracious!" Honest!

Red beans with rice counted among Louis Armstrong's favorite dishes. Many a time he ended his letters with "Red beans and ricely yours," and one finds allusions to this savory dish in several of his recordings. In his first version of *When It's Sleepy Time Down South* (Okeh), which begins with a dialogue between Louis and his pianist, Charlie Alexander, two New Orleans children meet up North. After the usual salutations, Louis states, "I'm goin' back home, those red beans 'n' pig ears, get a load of it." In the second version of *You Rascal You* (Decca) the menacing voice of Louis Armstrong can be heard reproaching the "rascal" for having eaten all his red beans and rice.

In Chicago, Louis formed a new band with Zilmer Randolph as leader, Budd Johnson on tenor saxophone, Keg Johnson on trombone, and eight other musicians; Teddy Wilson, at that time little known, was his pianist for some time. He did another tour through the United States before embarking by himself for Europe in July, 1933.

This time Louis Armstrong did not play England only. After having made himself heard in London and other cities, with a black band which had come from Paris as on the first visit, he went to the Scandinavian countries in October and November, where his previous successes were surpassed, or so it seemed to him. In Copenhagen especially, the welcome was astonishing. Louis says in *Swing That Music*, "The Copenhagen newspapers said that ten thousand people greeted us at the station. All I remember is a whole ocean of people all breaking through the police lines and bearing down on us until I got afraid we were going to get stomped underfoot. They pushed a big trumpet, all made out of flowers, into my hands and put me in an open automobile and started a parade."

Next, Louis played in Holland and returned to England where he was again heard in various cities. In April, 1934, he was to have taken part in a big concert organized by *The Melody Maker* (an English paper) with Coleman Hawkins, the great saxophonist recently arrived from the United States, but following unexplained differences the concert was canceled at the last moment.

During the summer of 1934 Louis moved into a furnished apartment in the rue de la Tour d'Auvergne in Paris, where he rested for two or three months. In November he gave two big concerts in the Salle Pleyel accompanied by black musicians then in Paris. There followed a tour of the provinces organized by his new manager, N. J. Canetti, and then he played in Italy. But once again his lips troubled him and the tour had to be interrupted. Canetti's lugubrious attitude induced Louis Armstrong to return to the United States the following January instead of prolonging his stay in Europe as he had intended.*

*"I will not come back here," he said. I refer to the matter in detail in my book *Twelve Years of Jazz—1927–1938*.

Louis Armstrong rested in Chicago until May. Then he formed an orchestra of fourteen musicians and made a tour of the Western and Southern states, going as far south as New Orleans and finishing in New York that September. Louis changed his musicians again; for the second time he adopted those of Luis Russell, who were to stay with him for many years. He played with this orchestra at Connie's Inn in New York from October 1935 on, and made many extensive tours throughout the United States in years that followed.

The year 1936 saw the publication of Louis Armstrong's first book, *Swing That Music*. Because of a poor childhood, Louis had received only a rudimentary education. But contrary to most black musicians for whom writing two lines is a tiresome task, Louis liked to send long letters to his friends, in a style that was entirely his own, the most perfect example of "spoken" style that I know. Louis not only wrote entirely as he spoke but he also created an entire system of punctuation establishing a rhythm which made his texts lively. There was no research on Louis' part; this was his natural style. It reflected this unique man's intense life. When he wrote Louis told what came into his mind with the same spontaneity as when he spoke. Here is a characteristic example taken from a letter which he addressed to me on April 14, 1936:

> Well! Well! Well, If it ain't a letter from my old Pal, old Gate Mouth, Louis (Satchmo) Armstrong. . . . Well, what do you know about that? . . . One thing I've always had it in my mind to write you first chance I'd get and now's the time, "Yessir" ee. . . . How are you these days, Pal'ly? . . . Are you having a good time? . . . I'll bet you, right now you're listening to some records. . . . Eh? . . . Yessir, I'll bet, you have your head real close by the Victrola, getting a

good load of whatever Band's playing, passing your opinion. . . .

This style of writing was so natural for him that he even composed telegrams in it. Instead of simply cabling: "Will arrive such-and-such a date at such-and-such a time. Best Wishes, Louis Armstrong," he would write: "Dear old pal, it's Friday that I will swing again my good old Selmer trumpet in New York. . . . Ha, ha, ha . . . Red beans and ricely yours . . . Louis (Satchmo) Armstrong." Louis told me that often the post office employees pointed out to him that by using such texts he would pay more dearly. But each time Louis would reply, "Send it as I've written it; I'll pay more, I prefer it this way."

Having received a typewriter as a present Louis found it amusing to use. When his mail was no longer enough to occupy him he set about writing his memoirs—and it is thus that his first book was born, *Swing That Music*. Unfortunately, Louis' business managers were stupid enough to fear that his unorthodox style of writing would harm the book's success. They corrected—or had corrected—the spicy style, suppressing his expressive punctuation and interjections. They removed everything from the text that gave it style and rhythm. Even more disturbing was that they added what they believed to be the essence of jazz and, worse still, they capitalized on the opportunity to exaggerate the merits of the Original Dixieland Jazz Band, which they represented as the first jazz orchestra. This crudely inaccurate assertion was made in an effort to revive this group by means of favorable publicity.

There remain, nevertheless, valuable descriptions of Louis Armstrong's childhood and adolescence, the most detailed being of great interest. But it would be naive to quote critical views of jazz itself as representative conceptions held by Louis.

One wonders perhaps why Louis permitted such liberties to be taken with his text. It would be judging the case of a black American musician with a twentieth-century European mentality accustomed to a certain respect for literature. Louis enjoyed writing his book, and then probably said to himself that corrections made by people more educated than he improved the draft. He never suspected they would have him say things he hadn't written, and it is unlikely that the revised text was ever submitted to him. Furthermore, due to the way blacks were regarded in the United States, Louis was certainly aware of the fact that he was not in a position to raise any objections and threw the whole thing out of his mind once the book was written.

But Louis Armstrong's personality emerges fairly well through this book nevertheless. One feels the intensity with which he lives each moment; one feels his innate goodness, his uprightness, his simplicity. Gifted with an extremely lively sensibility, his reactions are immediate and attractive in their finesse, spontaneity and intuition. He approaches people and things with his entire humanity. Though conscious of his talent he is not subject to pride because of it, but when he reacts sometimes violently against attack it is through wounded pride. He seems to have a great need for warmth and peace; he also shuns debate, useless complications and, like many black musicians, prefers to praise rather than criticize. If he has to express an opinion, he does so carefully, wary of attacking a musician or an orchestra by name. "You see," he told me one day, "I don't like giving my opinion of fellow members, I know very well that my remarks will exceed the aim and will go far, much too far. The little bit that

I have said will be distorted, enlarged, and will finish by hurting the person concerned because, coming from me, he will take things to heart, when he would not even have taken any notice coming from someone else. So, be very careful never to publish what I might tell you about a musician or about his music or style of playing. Keep everything that I say to you in this way between you and me."

If Louis speaks only circumspectly about the music of others—and even his own—it is not through indifference. On the contrary, music is such a natural part of him that he no longer feels the need to talk about it, just as one does not talk about the air one breathes. "When I was a kid," he said, "I would rather do without food than without music." He lived music every moment of his existence, practiced endlessly and created delightful music without even thinking about it. It was not only the moment he put the trumpet to his mouth or began to sing publicly that he became totally absorbed by music, but all day, in the street, at home, everywhere. Music was within him, and a melodic fragment was a voice speaking to him; a tune he caught or the mildest rhythm might rouse echoes in him, thrilling him to the depth of his subconscious. Alix Combelle, the French saxophonist, told me that during one of Louis' visits to Paris they were walking up the rue Pigalle late one night when a horse and carriage went by. The horse's hooves rang out clearly on the pavement and to the accompaniment of this unexpected rhythm, Louis immediately began to sing, to the great astonishment of his companion.

Between 1936 and 1939, Louis made seven trips to California but not only as a musician. Because his surprising talents as an actor had been noticed more and more, Hollywood had him appear in a number of films. The first was *Pennies from Heaven* with Bing Crosby, in which

Louis played *Skeleton in the Closet* with a small orchestra that included Lionel Hampton on drums. Then he was in *Artists and Models* with Jack Benny, where Louis played the trumpet wonderfully toward the end of the film. This sketch, alas, was completely cut out in the French version, which shows how ignorantly and arrogantly the public is often treated. Next came *Doctor Rhythm* with Bing Crosby (the scene in which Louis appeared was mysteriously cut from the versions shown in certain countries). Louis made a record of a number taken from that film, *The Trumpet Player's Lament.* Then there was *Everyday's a Holiday* with Mae West where Louis made a brief but brilliant appearance playing *Jubilee* (recorded on Decca). And *Goin' Places* with Dick Powell where Louis played and sang two numbers, notably, *Jeepers Creepers* (also issued on Decca). In this last film, Louis not only did a musical number but he had an actual part, even if it was far too modest for his ability. The inept process of dubbing robbed moviegoers of his voice and savory speech in the French version; fortunately his singing was not dubbed, as it was for other films!

Meanwhile, Louis had regained his old weight and it was a very plump man who was seen in *Artists and Models, Everyday's a Holiday,* and *Goin' Places;* although a few years older, he was the same Louis Armstrong of the 1927 and 1928 photographs.

Disconcerted by his new weight, Louis followed a strict diet during the war, one recommended by *Harper's Magazine,* and each morning on an empty stomach he took a glass of Pluto Water. His weight fell from 224 pounds to 184 and photos taken during this time resembled those of his European tour days. He was so pleased with his diet that he copied the recipe from *Harper's Magazine* and sent it to every one of his musical friends whom he had heard complaining about weight. At this time Louis Armstrong's letters finished with a new formula, "I'm Pluto Waterly yours."

During and after the war Louis Armstrong appeared in many films. Among others he was seen in *Jam Session* (with Ann Miller), *Atlantic City* (with Constance Moore), *Pillow to Post* (with Ida Lupino), and notably in *Cabin in the Sky* (M-G-M, 1943), a film which was entirely acted by blacks, with the incomparable singers and comedians Ethel Waters, Lena Horne, the great dancers Bubbles and Bill Bailey, and Duke Ellington's orchestra. It was one of the few interesting films ever made from the point of view of jazz.

In 1947 Louis Armstrong made *New Orleans* (United Artists), a film that should have been *his,* since it claimed to retrace the history of New Orleans jazz and its scenario somehow resembled Louis Armstrong's life story. Four of the six musicians recruited to surround him were, like himself, natives of Louisiana: Kid Ory, Barney Bigard, Bud Scott and Zutty Singleton. Jazz of a very high quality was heard in this film—when it was audible! For quite often the music faded out to allow for insipid dialogues delivered in an untalented way by the main white stars to support a dull, uninteresting plot. Then there were *A Song Is Born* (with Danny Kaye, 1948), *Courtin' Trouble* (with Jimmy Wakely), *Botta E Riposta (Je suis de la revue,* with Fernandel, 1950), *Here Comes the Groom* (with Bing Crosby, 1951), *The Strip* (with Mickey Rooney), *Glory Alley* (with Leslie Caron, 1952), *The Beat Generation* (with Steve Cochran, 1953).

1947 and the following years were bad for jazz. A national economic crisis closed many dance halls and cabarets which the United States government had increasingly taxed. Opportunities became fewer and many musicians were unemployed. Those most affected by the crisis were the big bands. There was not enough money to meet salary and transportation costs for bands of up to fifteen musicians. It was during 1947–1950 that nearly all big bands were forced to dissolve.

Without waiting for the situation to become any worse, Joe Glaser, Louis Armstrong's manager, broke up the big orchestra which Louis had headed for years. At the end of the spring of 1947 he surrounded the great trumpet player with a small group of brilliant soloists, for the most part very well chosen: Jack Teagarden (trombone), Barney Bigard (clarinet), Dick Cary (pianist), Arvell Shaw (string bass), Sidney Catlett (drums) and the singer and dancer Velma Middleton. When Earl Hines replaced Dick Cary in January, 1948, the group deserved the name which it had been given: the Louis Armstrong All Stars. During the following years the All Stars underwent personnel changes, but Louis was to continue to play with this group from then on. The group's instrumental composition (apart from the absence of a guitarist) was similar to the majority of bands of the New Orleans jazz period.

In 1948 Louis Armstrong returned to Europe for the first time since World War II—the occasion was the first international jazz festival, held in Nice, France, from February 22–28. In addition to Louis and his All Stars (Jack Teagarden, Barney Bigard, Earl Hines, Arvell Shaw, Big Sid Catlett, Velma Middleton), the festival featured Mezz Mezzrow's band (with, notably, Baby Dodds on drums and Pops Foster on bass), Rex Stewart's group, the Hot Club de France Quintet (with Django Reinhardt and Stephane Grappelly), and Claude Luter and his Lorientais among others.

This first festival exceeded even the most optimistic expectations for its success. Every evening people from all over Europe (they came by every means of transportation —even on bicycles) would crowd around these legendary musicians—especially around Louis Armstrong, who enjoyed an indescribable triumph, each evening signing hundreds of autographs on programs, papers, photos that were held out to him, even on people's hands and on the backs of women in evening gowns. It was delirious. Eighteen radio stations broadcast the concerts from day to day. At the end of this unforgettable week a *Vase de Sèvres* was presented from the President of the Republic to the *King of Jazz* amidst frantic applause from the crowd of diners and dancers gathered in the saloons of the Hôtel Negresco, where all the orchestras in the festival played in turn.

Before returning to the United States Louis Armstrong gave two concerts in Paris at the Salle Pleyel on March 2 and 3, 1948, to full houses. No less than 1,000 people had to be turned away from the second concert. Such a huge crowd was waiting for Louis Armstrong at the exit that Michel de Bry, in order to avoid the crush of admirers, made him escape into a police vehicle parked in front of the hall. The police vehicle pulled off immediately!

In whatever part of the world Louis played, human floods came to meet him. Several years later when he went to Brazil, hundreds of people broke through barriers and rushed toward him as he got off the plane. Fearing he would be injured, someone protected his face with a fencing mask! Even in New York he could no longer walk about without immediately being recognized and causing a crowd to gather.

In 1949 Louis received a different kind of honor from his home town during the famous Mardi Gras parade. He was named King of the Zulus and led the parade of the Zulus wending its way through various quarters of the town. Enthroned on top of a float, with his face made up and surrounded by his musicians, he threw coconuts which were painted with Zulu heads to passersby. It was on this occasion that he was named an honorary citizen of New Orleans. The Mayor handed him the keys to the city symbolized by a small gold key.

The following autumn Louis returned to Europe to play in France and several other countries. Because Sidney Catlett was ill, it was Cozy Cole who took over on drums in the All Stars. The tour was very tiring; rapid transportation was necessary to enable Louis Armstrong to cope with his tight schedule of performing in a different town each day all over Europe, often giving two concerts in each town. It was also necessary to fit in the official receptions Louis could not always avoid. While passing through Rome there was an invitation from Pope Pius XII for a private audience. He went with his wife,* saying to her, "I'll make the Pope laugh." When Pius XII, who spoke English fluently, asked him if he had any children, Louis replied, "No, your Holiness, but we keep tryin'." The Pope could not help smiling. . . .

It was during 1950 that Louis Armstrong began to write his autobiography, of which only the first volume has been published up to now. It first appeared in France (in the Juilliard editions) in 1952 under the title of *Ma Nouvelle Orleans*, translated by Madeleine Gautier from a photocopy of the manuscript typed by Louis Armstrong himself. This volume covers the first twenty-two years of his life and is the touching yet humorous story of his childhood and adolescence in New Orleans. It also depicts with

*Pretty Lucille Wilson, whom he had known when she was a chorus girl at the Cotton Club and whom he had married in Chicago in September, 1942. She is his present wife.

an alert pen several musicians of the earliest jazz period. It is written with a lot of life in a "spoken" style which is intensely rhythmic. The typewritten manuscript contained many ellipses which were like the text's respiration. The publisher asked that this punctuation be omitted from the French edition. The American edition did not appear until two years later, under the title *Satchmo—My Life in New Orleans.* Unfortunately, it was thought a good idea in this edition to tone down the style by rewriting Louis' manuscript. However, this was done without taking the multiple liberties which had disfigured *Swing That Music*, his first book. Ironically enough, the French translation is the better edition and the more faithful to the original manuscript. The book was subsequently translated into German and various other languages.

Louis would have continued writing his memoirs but countless tours did not yet allow him time to finish the second volume.

In 1951 Earl Hines and Jack Teagarden and then Barney Bigard left the band. When Louis Armstrong went to Europe for an extended tour in 1952 it was with the All Stars, including Trummy Young, the ex-trombonist of Jimmie Lunceford's orchestra, clarinet player Bob McCracken, and pianist Marty Napoleon, while Arwell Shaw and Cozy Cole remained in the rhythm section.

The following European tour in 1955 was a triumph. This time the orchestra was composed of Trummy Young (trombone), Edmund Hall (clarinet), Billy Kyle (piano), Arwell Shaw (bass), and Barrett Deems (drums). When Louis played for three weeks at the Olympia in Paris he was more exciting than ever. He had kept as his signature tune *When It's Sleepy Time Down South* and played it with some variation. However, instead of finishing normally, at the end of the number he launched into "Good evening everybody" or "Good night everybody" that each time caused a tremor of joy to flow through the audience. During thirty or so performances at the Olympia, this warm greeting varied according to circumstances. For example, if between two performances he was invited to a friend's house, he would add "Cassoulet is waiting," or any other appropriate remark. The so-called "specialized" press complained that Louis Armstrong "was giving way to Uncle Tomism"! But that accusation did not affect his success.

If we were to believe a mad press, there were incidents wherever Louis Armstrong appeared, broken seats, etc., as if jazz in general and Louis Armstrong especially made the fans go out of their minds. During the European tour of 1955 there was really only one incident, in Hamburg, and neither jazz nor Louis had anything to do with it. Here is what happened: the German impresario's failure to deliver the band to the hall on time for the matinee concert resulted in a curtailed performance. The audience was forcibly made to vacate the building in order to allow in those waiting for the evening show which took place immediately afterward. Fire hoses were used and one can imagine the disturbance that ensued! The incident proved an ideal topic for journalists seeking sensational news. The incident in Hamburg had become a riot. As nothing sensational happened in France it was necessary to resort to subterfuge. At Roubaix while students were crying "encore" and gesticulating, a photographer caught the scene while a newspaper reporter urged some students to feign a brawl.

The tours continued throughout the world. In December, 1956, a benefit concert was given at the Royal Festival Hall in London for Hungarian refugees, when Louis was accompanied by the Royal Philharmonic Orchestra; in 1957 it was Accra, Ghana, where he played before more than five thousand people.

All this shows that Louis was hardly able to spend more than a few days a year at his comfortable home in Corona, Long Island. So he had his way of making himself at home wherever he went. Definite instructions were given to his valet, Dr. Pugh, to have at each hotel the contents of the twenty-four suitcases which formed Louis Armstrong's personal baggage consistently arranged in the same order and position as the day before, including two tape recorders (in case one broke down); a transistor radio, the medicine box, and other objects were made readily available.

Louis couldn't exist without music, and it was rare for one of the two tape recorders not to be playing, even if there were visitors. He would follow everything simultaneously and thoroughly. In the same way that Louis could follow two conversations at the same time, he could do two different things at the same time such as write on a train while noticing the countryside; or sleep at the dentist's, to whom he would say after opening his mouth, "Wake me up when it's finished." For if Louis Armstrong got little sleep—at least little at one stretch—he could fall asleep at will, and soon after settling down his muscles would relax and he would be asleep.

His medicine case contains the best medicines that Louis has discovered during his travels for effectively treating all types of ailments; medicines for throat illnesses, strained eyes, attacks of toothache, for care of the lips, laxatives (the famous Swiss Kriss with a basis of herbs that all his friends have had to try willy-nilly), and not forgetting a gargle of his own concoction which he uses with a flourish. He begins in the usual way, then starts to pluck the skin under his chin and on his neck, so that the liquid can reach the remotest parts of his throat. When he thinks the operation has lasted long enough to clear his throat, he spits out the liquid and to demonstrate success releases a superb "Oh, yes!" with arms outstretched exactly as if on stage.

What Louis Armstrong is in everyday life, he transposes for his shows. Being a keen observer, he is also gifted with a sort of infallibility for tastefully introducing sage remarks he has noted and retained, which add spontaneity to the spectacular quality of Louis Armstrong concerts. On the whole Louis knows everything that is not learned in school, whatever the school. He has learned everything the hard way from life, from observing it. That is why nothing he does seems to have been studied—yet nothing, however, is left to chance. The self-discipline which frames his creative genius is so well integrated that it is difficult to differentiate between his work and his daily life.

He hardly ever talks about himself; and the memories that he recalls with friends often portray a past which he treats with indifference, humor and laughter, as though it were irrelevant. One day he told about one of the first concerts he had given in England. His wife was creating a jealous scene in his dressing room. Absolutely furious, she was looking for any means to make Louis miss his entry onto the stage, heaping him with insults, even trying to punch him on the lips. "You realize," Louis commented, "that's the worst thing that could happen to a trumpet player. Meanwhile I heard the theater fellow shouting, 'Mr. Armstrong, on stage in two minutes.' So here's what I did. With a mighty punch I knocked her out and then I laid her down on the couch and got out fast." The audience saw him enter, all smiles, uttering his customary "Yeah!"

He overflows with naturalness, his *own* naturalness,

without egotism or vanity, treating equally the great ones of this world and the dressing room attendants, poor friends and rich friends, with a politeness molded and refined by his intensely human relationship with his fellow man.

It seems that Louis Armstrong has always shown a distinct preference for women with very dark skin, for each of his four wives has been dark in color. "The blacker the berry the sweeter the juice," Louis said, according to an old proverb.* One day he stated, "To live with me a woman must adopt my way of life, respect my syllabus, believe in me; her way of thinking, her sensibility, the way in which her heart is moved are, for me, questions of prime importance, and above all, she must move me."

With a word or two, he can redeem any situation, whatever it is. In 1957, during a concert he was giving at Knoxville, Tennessee, before an audience composed of two-thirds whites and one-third blacks, two or three sticks of dynamite were thrown into the entrance hall to protest this integrated concert. While no one was injured, the noise was enough to frighten the audience. A panic was feared. Motioning to the musicians to continue playing, Louis put down his trumpet and said, "O.K. folks, it's my private telephone that's just rung," and immediately started playing again.

As for racial issues Louis Armstrong has never wanted to get mixed up with them: "My trumpet doesn't have to bother with that for the good reason that it doesn't know anything about it. I play and I will play wherever people want to listen to me."

*"It was love at first sight with Lucille because of the color of her skin. When she danced at the Cotton Club she was the darkest in the company," Louis explained.

However, at the time of school desegregation efforts in Little Rock, Arkansas, in 1957, Louis Armstrong did not hesitate to treat Governor Faubus as an uneducated plowboy and to give President Eisenhower some home truths. He refused the State Department's offer to make a propaganda tour of Russia. "I know that this racial hatred which is appearing in the South is above all the act of a minority; it's the stupidest white class who are making all this noise. If I go to Russia one day, it will be under my own name, for if I go under an official title, they'll ask me what I think of all this Little Rock business and what do you want me to reply?"

Louis' entourage was terrified by these declarations and, judging them too violent, tried to put a damper on the matter. His road manager called up the press while Louis slept and stated Louis was not as angry as all that, that he could not be cross for more than a few seconds and that, besides, Louis had said that Mr. Eisenhower had done more for Negroes than his two predecessors. When he discovered what had been said in his name, Louis called the press to his hotel lounge in Chicago; and with his musicians standing at his side as a sign of solidarity, he asserted again "that the Government could go to the devil with its plans for a propaganda tour of Soviet Russia." He added, "My road manager especially doesn't like Negroes and is trying to make me look a fool beside people of my race. I'm perfectly capable of speaking for myself; I am fighting in favor of my rights. As for my road manager, he knows nothing about music; he used to be a truck driver."

In 1960 the State Department organized an Armstrong tour in Africa "in order to strengthen the friendship between the United States and the new African States." "What are you going to try and prove to the Africans?" a journalist asked him. "Me? Nothing at all. I'm going there to blow my trumpet. I don't have anything to do with politics, I know nothing about it. My life is my trumpet and my music, that's all."

This triumphant and often picturesque tour lasted several months during which Louis gave more than forty concerts and covered nearly 37,500 miles, excluding South Africa where for "unknown reasons" (in fact, not so much so . . .), the tour was canceled at the last moment. The tour was made in two parts: first from October to the beginning of December, then, after a month's stay in Paris to make a film, continued during most of January, 1961. It was during January while at Freetown in Sierra Leone that the All Stars singer Velma Middleton fell seriously ill. Taken to the town's hospital, she died there the following February 9th. Velma had been a perfect partner for Louis Armstrong. Each of their duets was a masterpiece and a musical sketch such as blacks enjoy and perform. Sudden outbursts, mimicry, and exchanges rebounded between them with maximum effect.

The film made in December, 1960, *Paris Blues* (with Sidney Poitier and Paul Newman) was not too successful despite the stars who were in it and Duke Ellington's music. Nothing could save a dull scenario. It ran only a few weeks.

It was not until April, 1961, that the other illustrious jazzman, Duke Ellington, recorded two entire LPs with the King of Jazz. Duke, who was asked one day what he considered the predominant influence in the history of jazz, replied, "Louis Armstrong—at both ends." The seventeen numbers recorded by Louis and his All Stars with Duke on the piano were all Duke's compositions and Louis had never played most of them. "What struck me," stated Stanley Dance, who was present at this memorable meeting, "was the fantastic swiftness with which Louis

Armstrong makes himself master of a number and of the words. He read the words once and began to sing them, giving them maximum expression."

Louis has also recorded with stars whose music has no relation to his own. That is why Louis Armstrong's name is coupled on a microgroove album with that of the progressive Dave Brubeck. The album's music by Dave Brubeck, and the words by Mrs. Brubeck, were so heavy with pedantic politico-philosophical allusions that at the end of the session Louis felt the need to relax and began to tell some of those extravagant inexhaustible stories—which emerge once the hard work is finished—while at the same time folding up his things.

Whenever he can, Louis seizes moments from a crushing schedule of obligations as a musician and a world-wide star, to relax with his own people. He has never permitted himself to be uprooted, nor to become a sacred cow. He has never let himself be cut off from his milieu, from the social ground where he has roots. "When I think," his personal manager once said, "that Louis could associate with the nobles of this world, and he continues being happy with all those bums, I can't understand it!"

Snobbery is an unknown feeling for him; and his generosity is without bounds. His wallet is open to all those who are in need, even to scroungers whom he knows for what they are. But it doesn't matter, for he likes spreading happiness.

His memory for faces is amazing. He remembers the most humble as well as the most important, and although he sees many people, he immediately recognizes them. One day in Paris after a concert at Pleyel had finished, Louis was in his dressing room taking his usual time to change, and attending to his hands and face. Time was getting on, and the caretaker began to bewail the fact that she had missed the last Métro and now in order to get home would have to pay taxi fare. Louis, hearing voices, asked what was happening; it was explained to him. Louis took a large note from his wallet, called the caretaker and gave it to her, telling her not to worry about the subway she had missed, that she now had the means to go home by taxi. The woman thanked him, smiled, and returned quietly to her corner. The noise had stopped. A year later, Louis was again playing Pleyel and the same caretaker was there at her job. As soon as Louis saw her on entering the artists' foyer, he pointed at her and burst out laughing, "Ha, ha, ha, ha, . . . No subway for you tonight—taxi!"

In December, 1963, Louis made a record that was to take the whole world by storm, *Hello, Dolly!* On Broadway, in Harlem, in all of New York and its surrounding districts, people listened to the strain of Louis Armstrong's trumpet blowing through loudspeakers in all the supermarkets, juke boxes, and bars. *Hello, Dolly!* was played on the radio up to 10,000 times a day, on all the stations. At each one of his concerts Louis had to play it three or four times more as an encore. There was a sigh of joy in performance halls when the first bars of this were heard, and it was requested everywhere.

Pops, as Louis is known to his friends, had never played the same number so often. So in order to avoid the monotony which repetition might cause, Louis created *totally* different variations each time. Jack Bradley and Roni Failows, fans of Louis Armstrong who did not miss a single one of his concerts in the New York region, noted that by recording several LPs of different versions of *Hello, Dolly!* he produced extraordinarily varied music. From this, one can see the inexhaustible genius of Louis' invention.

For his first performance of *Hello, Dolly!* in France,

Pops skillfully inserted a musical quotation from the *Marseillaise* in the seventeenth bar of his trumpet chorus. What similar allusions would not be discovered if one had recordings of all Louis' innumerable versions of *Hello, Dolly!*

Apparently the jazz critics did not notice this, since they frequently complained that Louis Armstrong "continually repeated this tune from a musical comedy." Some journalists went so far as to ask Pops, "How can you, a jazz musician, play a number like *Hello, Dolly!* which is only a pop tune?" Louis readily replied, "It's not the number that counts, it's the way you play it; that's what makes jazz." He could have added, *Tea for Two, Hallelujah, Sometimes I'm Happy,* and many other numbers which jazz musicians have included in their repertoire for a quarter of a century. These were all originally simple pop tunes like *Hello, Dolly!*

During the past fifteen years, Louis Armstrong has taken part in various films, without ever having had a role worthy of his acting talents. He made *The Glenn Miller Story* (with James Stewart, 1954), *High Society* (with Grace Kelly, 1956), *Jazz on a Summer's Day* (1959), *The Five Pennies* (with Danny Kaye), and *When the Boys Meet the Girls* (with Connie Francis, 1965). In 1966 there was *A Man Called Adam* with music by Benny Carter, and the principal role was given to Sammy Davis, Jr., who on viewing the film exclaimed, "I am there to give the maximum in front of the camera because I'm the star, and then a big pan of Louis Armstrong's face appears and it becomes Louis Armstrong's film!" And in 1968 there appeared the film version of the musical comedy *Hello, Dolly!* starring Barbra Streisand. Louis had the short role of a band leader.

Louis Armstrong returned to France several times during the 1960s. In 1962, he went twice and his concerts at the Olympia were wonderful. The audience had not only grown bigger, but it had changed. It now included all the teenage fans of Johnny Halliday who dressed like him, wore the same hair style, and listened to Louis Armstrong in almost religious silence. Now at last the press changed its tune: there was no more question of Louis' age, even less his "decline." "If Armstrong is grandfather's jazz, then bravo and thanks again," one read in *L'Aurore*. Michel Perrin hit the nail on the head in *Les Nouvelles Littéraires* with his usual accuracy: "After the forced publicity, the young people discovered the tree of life: this face where all the troubles and all the joys of a race are inscribed, this body in which every molecule dances, these golden notes that Armstrong seems to hold in the sky before drawing them out from his trumpet." Only those gentlemen, the "specialist critics" persisted soullessly. "I was rather bored," said one. "It does not really come from the heart," said another. "It's sentimentality made to order," said a third. But no one paid any attention to what they wrote.

The year 1965 saw Louis again in Paris at the Palais des Sports, where the acoustics are, alas, calamitous. In 1967, he made his first appearance at the Antibes Festival on the French Riviera. Louis had been ill several months before and this short but extremely busy European tour proved to be very hard on a man hardly out of convalescence. In Antibes Louis was his usual grand self for the second concert.

In autumn 1968 Louis fell ill again. At the moment I am writing these lines he has not resumed his musical activities and is writing his memoirs at home in Corona.*

*Since the summer of 1970, Louis Armstrong is back on the mound with TV appearances, recordings, engagements in cabarets, such as in Las Vegas, etc. *Quel homme!!*

At the end of 1965 all of America celebrated the fiftieth anniversary of the King of Jazz's professional career. In 1968 he took part in the first Jazz Festival in his home town, New Orleans, where his first cornets and trumpets are now on display at the Jazz Museum. All over the world the press sings the praises of this unique man. One article summed it up this way: "The warmest sound, the friendliest in the world is to hear Louis Armstrong say 'Yeah!' "

1. Louis, Chicago, circa 1934.

2. Party honoring Louis and Duke Ellington, Chicago, 1935. Left to right: Duke Ellington (fifth from left); Louis' third wife Alpha; Herb Morand (standing with trumpet); Joe Lindsay (standing to right of man with top hat); Clarence Armstrong, Louis' adopted son (to right of seated woman); Wellman Braud; Art Stewart, president of Chicago musicians union.

3. RIGHT. A rare, previously unpublished photo of Louis (second from left) and his adopted son Clarence (far right), Chicago, circa 1926.

4. BELOW. Louis Armstrong and his Stompers, Sunset Cafe, Chicago, 1927. Left to right: Earl Hines, Peter Briggs, Honoré Dutry, Armstrong, Bill Wilson, Tubby Hall, Arthur Bassett, Boyd Atkins, Joe Walker, Al Washington, Willard Hamby.

5. ABOVE. Louis Armstrong Orchestra, Chicago, 1937. Left to right: Henry "Red" Allan, J. C. Higginbotham, Louis Bacon, George Washington, Shelton Hemphill, Jimmy Archey, Luis Russell, Sonny Wood, Paul Barbarin, Louis, female vocalist, Albert Nicholas, Lee Blair, Charlie Holmes, Pops Foster, Pete Clark, Bingie Madison.

6. BELOW. Louis with Edward "Kid" Ory. When King Oliver left New Orleans to work in Chicago, Louis replaced him in Kid Ory's band. Eight years later, Ory was recording with Louis' Hot Five and Hot Seven in Chicago.

7. ABOVE. Louis and his long-time drummer Big Sid Catlett, circa 1940.

8. A rare piece of sheet music with photo of Louis as he appeared with Les Hite and his California Syncopators. When Louis joined this band in Los Angeles in 1930, the name was changed to Louis Armstrong and his Sebastian New Cotton Club Orchestra as they were appearing at Frank Sebastian's Cotton Club. This band recorded a dozen memorable sides for Okeh records from July, 1930, to March, 1931. Kneeling in front is Les Hite, apparently serenading Louis. Of particular note is seventeen-year-old Lionel Hampton at the drums. It was during this time that Lionel played his first recorded vibe solo—on Louis' 1930 recording of *Memories of You.* Also in this band is Marshall Royal on alto (directly behind Hite). He has been musical director of Count Basie's band for the past twenty years. Another famous face is that of trombonist Lawrence Brown (far right)—a mainstay of Duke Ellington for thirty years.

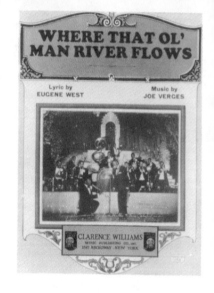

9. LEFT. Cover of rare music folio of 50 Hot Choruses, which Louis recorded on cylinder for Melrose in Chicago in 1926. The solos were then transcribed and published in this book.

Part Two
THE STYLE

. . . graceful and easy but still full of power and drive.

MILTON "MEZZ" MEZZROW, *Really the Blues*.

Louis Armstrong is unique as a musician for three reasons: instrumental technique, creativeness, and as a "jazz" musician. The three elements form a whole that cannot be dissociated. In order to bring Louis Armstrong's musicianship even better to the fore I shall analyze them one by one.

As an instrumentalist, nobody can be compared to Louis. There are of course many trumpet virtuosi in jazz, but none plays the instrument so perfectly as Louis. There certainly are trumpet players such as Rex Stewart, Roy Eldridge, Charlie Shavers, Dizzy Gillespie, Clark Terry and Harry James who can play phrases as fast and vertiginously as Louis does. There are others who can play higher notes. But when it comes to the perfect trumpet technique one cannot judge a musician by high notes or speed only. High notes depend partly on the mouthpiece used. A special mouthpiece can help a musician blow high notes but it may well be to the detriment of the lower registers; and if acrobatic trumpet players can play higher notes than Louis it is often because of the mouthpiece used (with few exceptions like Cat Anderson). Yet Louis Armstrong never wished to sacrifice the lower registers to the high one, and his playing is more perfect than that of anyone else in *all* ranges of the instrument. On the other hand, Louis never wanted to sacrifice the tonal quality of the notes to their height, and his high G's are so full and so mellow that other trumpets' high G's usually sound like squeaks in comparison.

Louis is also a very fast trumpet player. If he is not as well known for speed as a Rex Stewart or a Harry James it is because Louis is not especially interested in such effects. Also, one cannot play trumpet as fast as, for instance, a clarinet without sacrificing some of its tonal quality. Tone is precisely what Louis Armstrong specially prizes. Ultra-fast solos by Dizzy Gillespie may be technical *tours de force*, but they nevertheless deprive the trumpet of many of its special characteristics.

Even if certain trumpet players are faster than Louis Armstrong, or can hit higher notes, or have more volume, nothing would change the fact that, generally speaking, Louis plays the trumpet and "fills his horn" better than anybody else. He is the only one to possess *simultaneously* all possible qualities: an easy, beautiful tone in all registers, versatility, a most beautiful attack, perfect accuracy, poignant vibrato, volume, density of sound, perfect legato and staccato playing, and amazing flexibility of the lips for inflections. This enables Louis to make his trumpet sing as no other instrumentalist can, to blow his horn with such mastery that his subtlety of expression is comparable only to that of his own voice when he sings. His horn is not (as to other trumpet players) something exterior to him. It is part of him and sounds like his own voice. He does not give so much the impression of playing the trumpet as of singing through it. The same can be said of Louis Armstrong's vibrato. His vibrato does not sound merely instrumental, but as if his whole person were vibrating. That is the reason one single note played by Louis Armstrong makes all the other instrumentalists forgettable.

Reaching higher notes or playing faster runs are technical exploits that belong to a good athletic performance rather than to the proper technique of the instrument. What counts first is to be able to phrase with the same fullness of sound in all registers with an equally clear, clean articulation, and with constant ease and accuracy. Louis Armstrong is the master of all that. His instrumental technique is not an acrobatic performance; it is entirely devoted to music.

Physically, Louis Armstrong has the characteristics of a good trumpet player. His prominent lips (he was nicknamed "Satchelmouth") are so supple they stretch effortlessly at his command to play high notes. Very often he will start a chorus by hitting a high note as if it were the easiest thing to do, instead of reaching it progressively. This causes a terrific pressure on the labial muscles and the imprint of the mouthpiece remains in evidence on his lips. His thorax is broad, which enables him to blow his horn with extraordinary power. He can fill his lungs with surprising quantities of air, which allows him to play for an extended amount of time before taking another breath. The trumpet is the hardest of all instruments to play, the one which demands the greatest physical effort of the lips, lungs, and heart. Joe Oliver used to say, "You'll never get the trumpet, she'll get you." Louis Armstrong is the only trumpet player to have successfully resisted the harmful effects of the strain for more than fifty years.

For invention, Louis is also incomparable. In all his solos of all periods he constantly creates, and his inventiveness is so genuine that Louis seems the very incarnation of jazz music. His sense of harmony enables him to embroider any number with amazing ease—good, mediocre, or bad though the melody may be. Louis is so gifted melodically that each of his solos is a world of musical beauty. Sometimes his melodic line is uncomplicated, sometimes most intricate and subtle, and sometimes he combines both within the same solo. The beauty of his phrases impressed jazz musicians so much that most of them modeled their style on Louis'. The whole of jazz music was transformed by Louis, overthrown by his genius. In Louis Armstrong's music is the New Orleans style at its peak, and also the basis of almost all styles that were derived from it, directly or indirectly. And Louis Armstrong cannot be held responsible for the tastelessness of some of his imitators. Blame must be put on those disciples. When it is a question of imitating or influencing, the style of the master shows the way, but it cannot be as vital as the personality of the disciple. One is inspired by the musician whose nature is most like one's own; yet disciples of the same master may obtain vastly different or even opposite results. Both were inspired by Louis Armstrong, but Sidney De Paris had a very well-balanced style, while Henry Allen's was sometimes erratic; yet both musicians were imitating the same Louis at the same period. The same phenomenon can be noted among musicians who came after Louis. Roy Eldridge influenced both an extravagant trumpet player like Dizzy Gillespie, and Harry Edison, whose trumpet playing is remarkably neat and well balanced. The fact is that Gillespie developed the awkward and complicated side of Roy's style while Edison drew from what Roy was doing the best jazz qualities.

Louis Armstrong was the first to use in his variations on a theme those altered notes that began to proliferate during the '30s. I don't mean the altered notes that belong to the very essence of jazz music and come from the blues (3rd and 7th degrees of the scale flattened—blue notes). Louis Armstrong has been using them like any other black musician. I mean other alterations. Altered notes belonging to the black music tradition were heard only in the many inflections of their singing. Louis Armstrong is the one who put them in the instrumental idiom; and it is he who dared put them right into his trumpet phrases instead of inserting or resolving them in the form of inflections. As far back as 1926 or 1927 those altered notes can be heard in Louis' records and not in any other recording of the time. Listen to Louis' solos on *Wild Man Blues,* or *Twelfth Street Rag,* or *Chicago Breakdown,* for instance. Later on Louis would use such altered notes increasingly, but always with much taste and accuracy. In Louis' music those notes mean something. They fit into the context, in the melodic line, and help make the solos sing magnificently. They spring up so naturally and logically that you hardly notice them. Instead of shocking like something out of place, they underline the development of a melody.

Some so-called modern musicians were to use altered notes like automatons. Many younger musicians put altered notes in their solos, not to follow the flood of inspiration but because it had become a system they depended on. The presence of those notes in their solos is what some people have called "progress" in jazz music. The more altered notes and the fewer fundamental notes you play, the more modern you are supposed to be. Such childish theorists do not realize that building an entire chorus upon altered notes is just a matter of habit and does not imply any musical superiority. Besides—and this is even more important—the more altered notes, the less effective they become, so that the purpose is lost. "Boredom was born of uniformity." In music, as in all arts, everything is a matter of relationship. In Louis' solos, altered notes get their full meaning from their relationship with unaltered notes. When altering notes becomes a system, the relationship between notes makes the entire thing just as dull as if the notes were not altered.

So it is not a matter of using altered notes or not, but a way of connecting the notes so that the phrase will sound pretty and the melodic line will keep singing. This can be done with any kind of note, altered or not. Louis Armstrong felt it. To build a chorus he may use either two or three notes or a multitude of them, offering the most original and unexpected relationship.

Louis Armstrong's music is full of melody. He loves melody. He always keeps the melodic line in sight; the harmonic basis remains for him a consequence of the melody. That is why he can casually and slightly paraphrase on a theme or create a series of variations on it which depart from the theme but still make a melody, only a different one.

In contrast many self-styled modern trumpet players do not bother with the theme they have to play. They have their eye on only the harmonic basis and start improvising on it with such a number of altered notes that the melody is gone and nobody knows what number they are playing. There stands the difference between performance and inspired music.

Louis Armstrong often declared in interviews that it was no longer possible to get back to New Orleans jazz as it was played in the beginning, a most realistic and wise statement. But Louis also said, "The more jazz music gets away from the New Orleans spirit, the less authentic it is."

All his life Louis Armstrong has encouraged young musicians of talent, those with something to say that is their own. But when "be bop" took over, Louis soon after declared in plain words that it was no longer jazz. He explained why very clearly to Barry Ulanov (*Metronome*, April, 1945):

> You know what King Oliver said to me? "You gotta play that lead sometimes. Play the melody, play the lead and learn." And that's what I like to hear, sometimes, anyway. Some of that fantastic stuff, when they tear out from the first note and you ask yourself, "What the hell's he playing?"—that's not for me. Personally, I wouldn't play that kinda horn if I played a hundred years; you don't have to worry about me stealing those riffs.

With "fantastic stuff," Louis is taking care of those modern trumpet players who puff up their runs with altered notes, preferably in the high register, playing as fast as they can with no melody whatsoever coming through. Nothing of the sort with Louis Armstrong. Whenever he plays, whatever number he improvises on, the musical line always shines with clarity. The variations, far from being erratic or careless, develop with logical assurance and perfect mastery. Louis never gropes; the notes appear to come under his command effortlessly. His imagination is limitless. They never knew what Louis would play next, although they could have been a little blasé where Louis' invention was concerned. Yet they were still bewildered like Lawrence Brown, for instance, who explains his admiration, "Those were wonderful nights playing with Louis. Each night found us perched on the edge of our seats, breathlessly waiting to hear what Louis was going to play next. We were as excited and certainly more frantic than the paying customers."*

Louis Armstrong is *the* jazz musician *par excellence*. Jazz music stands primarily on swing, that subdued and regular pulse which brings life to the musical frame. The way Louis Armstrong swings is phenomenal; it beats that of all other musicians. His very style favors the pulse. Just as he takes care of his tone (the prettiest trumpet tone there is) and keeps a keen eye on the melody, so he wants the singing quality of his music to stay well attached to the pulse-beat, whether he sings or plays the trumpet. His phrasing is as perfect rhythmically as it is melodically. In that also, Louis Armstrong proves himself an accomplished musician. Whatever he plays is so neat, so well cut, so straightforward that it sings and swings to the utmost.

When musicians get too involved in harmonic research and look mostly for complicated phrases, they are bound to lose a lot in regard to the pulse. Complication in jazz music, as in many forms of art, is the enemy, the more so with jazzmen who look for swing first. It may even happen that overcomplicated soloists get in the way of the rhythm section and restrain the pulse of a whole band. Louis cooperates with the pulse of the drums. He plays with the rhythm section, carrying it on as much as it supports him. His phrases have a beat and they sing at the same time.

Of course, when Louis Armstrong plays sinuous, intricate and fast phrases, the pulse is more subdued, but it is still there because he has his own methods of execution that make his music bubble with swing. One of the proceedings consists of large, flexible notes played glissando. I do not mean the ordinary glissandos used by trombone players ever since jazz was born, but more subtle and

Metronome, May, 1945.

imaginative inflections, with a progression as if the sound were held back and then hurried out in turn. All the efficiency of such inflections lies in the suppleness of execution, on how strong and expressive they can be because of flexibility. Numerous instrumentalists have adoped that way of expression from Louis Armstrong, but none has obtained the same swinging result.

Louis Armstrong also makes extensive use of rubato (a musical procedure consisting of modifying the length of the notes when stating the melody, attacking the note later than expected or making one note longer, the other shorter, or vice versa). It is so natural for Louis to use rubato that it is hardly noticeable in his playing unless you try to play or sing as he does while listening to his records.

Louis' vibrato is exceptionally moving and swinging. Most delicate when it starts, the note vibrates more and more until the end, and then comes out with dramatic intensity. The very essence of Louis' personality shows in his vibrato. That is where one feels his soul.

Louis' powerful way of hitting a note or having it vibrate is an enchantment for the listener because the power accompanies deep emotion and profound feeling. Louis' sound is never brutal or hoarse, as Roy Eldridge's sometimes becomes. Nor is it as sweet as that of a Joe Smith or a Harold Baker, who do not show the biting accent, that take-it-or-leave-it touch that sends the listener. Many a musician has tried to acquire the same double virtue of Louis Armstrong's intonations. And quite a few have succeeded more or less, such as Tommy Ladnier, Jonah Jones, Cootie Williams and Charlie Shavers, but even the strongest could not reach the same intensity.

All that has been said about the trumpet player can be said of the singer. Louis blows his horn exactly as he sings

—and vice versa. It is just a matter of means; the trumpet, the voice.

Louis has a small harsh voice and needs a mike, but the timbre is beautiful and moving. Louis' singing has inspired not only singers but instrumentalists as well. A whole brass or reed section can phrase an arrangement or cut the sound abruptly in the same way that Louis Armstrong has been singing for over fifty years.

The most notable difference between Louis' singing and playing comes because of the words, for there is a rhythm to watch in the words that differs from the rhythm attached to the notes. There is also the meaning of the words involved. Creative as he is, Louis Armstrong, when he sings, will add some words here and cut some there in order to give the lyrics their fullest meaning and pulse. He brings so much life, beauty and joy to whatever he sings and does it with such ease, that one feels he has just invented the lyrics of the song and sings them for you alone.

Louis Armstrong sings his heart out with all the vigor and tenderness within his soul to express all human feelings with the most accomplished artistry. His music identifies with the soul of the black. No wonder, therefore, that all blacks and so many whites opened their hearts to all that Louis Armstrong had to say.

Jazz musicians are unanimous in recognizing Louis' genius and influence. To quote but one, Roy Eldridge once declared that nobody will exercise the influence Louis Armstrong had on trumpet style; that his tone, his phrasing, and his power had never been equalled, and that Louis was the first modern jazzman. Coming from the musician who had the biggest subsequent influence on trumpet players after Louis himself, such a statement means a lot.

Of course Louis Armstrong did not create everything. He unconsciously drew upon the black musical tradition and was consciously inspired by a few trumpet players of the first great jazz generation, mainly by Joe "King" Oliver. There were great jazz musicians before Louis such as Jelly Roll Morton, King Oliver, Sidney Bechet, James P. Johnson. Yet it is thanks to Louis Armstrong's music that the majority of the jazzmen began to stand up for themselves. There is the shape of jazz as it existed before Louis Armstrong, and the transformed shape after his advent. Quite naturally, the most noticeable influence of Louis Armstrong has been on trumpet players.

Musicians playing in apparently opposite styles have taken from the same common source. Muggsy Spanier, Max Kaminsky, and numerous other trumpet players imitated the classic New Orleans style of Louis' 1922–1927 period. Later, Sidney de Paris, Cootie Williams, Lips Page, Jonah Jones, Bill Coleman, Buck Clayton, and all the other great trumpet players would try to discover the secret of Louis' audacious and beautiful style. Each would take from Louis what he thought would fit his own personality best. Sidney de Paris would catch some of Louis' emotion; Jonah Jones, Louis' fire and mastery. Louis' mobility and biting execution would appeal to Bill Coleman, while Cootie Williams would impregnate his trumpet playing with Louis Armstrong's lift and his dense and full tone. The result was that although these last two musicians were influenced by the same Louis they sounded completely different from each other. Examples of this sort are endless.

Roy Eldridge, inspired as he was by many aspects of Rex Stewart, Coleman Hawkins, and Benny Carter, was nonetheless greatly inspired by Louis Armstrong, especially from the strict trumpet point of view. In his good solos at slow tempo, Roy has a dramatic and masterful accent which comes from Louis. The younger trumpets who were not directly inspired by Louis were indirectly influenced by him through Roy Eldridge.

When it comes to jazz singers it would be hard to name one who did not imitate Louis more or less: Ethel Waters, Billie Holiday, Ella Fitzgerald, Fats Waller, Taft Jordan, King Cole, how many others! Here again, the young have adopted Louis' style indirectly through such and such a singer who formed his style from the Louis Armstrong style.

Although it is not obvious, the fact is that Louis Armstrong shaped the style of other instrumentalists besides those on trumpet. On trombone, there are Jimmy Harrison, Jack Teagarden, Trummy Young, and their many disciples. Coleman Hawkins transformed his tenor saxophone style on slow tempos under the influence of Louis' fantastic trumpet solos of the 1929–1932 period. It is also Louis who enriched Earl "Fatha" Hines' musical personality. Earl himself is a model for many pianists. One can detect Louis' influence in the playing of the greatest guitar soloist, Django Reinhardt. You even find riffs, phrases created by Louis Armstrong, forming the basis of orchestrations for big bands, and arrangers have also been inspired by Louis' music. It is really Louis Armstrong who electrified and put on their own two feet, just about all the great jazzmen.

10. Louis and Bing with Lional Hampton on drums at left rear, 1936.

11. Louis as the devil's helper in M-G-M's film *Cabin in the Sky*, circa 1943.

12. ABOVE. Scene from United Artist 1946 movie *New Orleans*. Billie Holiday with Louis' last big band. Band includes bassist Arvell Shaw and trombonist "Big Chief" Russell Moore (far right).

13. BELOW. Louis Armstrong and his Orchestra, Chicago, 1931. From a 1931 movie. Left to right: Mike McKendrick (guitar), Al Washington (saxophone), Louis, John Lindsay (bass), Preston Jackson (trombone), George James (alto), Charlie Alexander (piano), Tubby Hall (drums), Zilmer Randolph (trumpet).

14. ABOVE. Scene from 1946 movie *New Orleans*. Charlie Beal (piano), Louis, unknown tenor, Barney Bigard (clarinet), Bud Scott (guitar), Zutty Singleton (drums), Mutt Carey (trumpet), Kid Ory (trombone), Red Callender (bass).

15. BELOW. Louis in scene from movie *Pennies from Heaven*.

16. Louis and band in scene from 1946 movie *New Orleans*. Rear: Louis, Kid Ory, Barney Bigard. Front: Bud Scott, Zutty Singleton, Charlie Beal, Red Callender.

17. ABOVE. Louis in Ghana — from *Satchmo the Great*, 1957. Louis and his wife Lucille, dancing with a couple of tribal chiefs.

18. BELOW. Louis and his vocalist Velma Middleton, who worked with his big band and All Stars for twenty years, until her death while touring Africa with the All Stars in the early 1960s.

19. Louis in classroom in Ghana, 1957.

20. ABOVE. Louis (center) as King of the Zulus, Mardi Gras, New Orleans, 1949.

21. BELOW. Louis, Jack Carter, Sheila and Gordon MacRae pose for publicity shot for ABC-TV special "Winter Carnival at Sun Valley."

Part Three
THE MUSIC OF
LOUIS ARMSTRONG
ON RECORDS

Louis really blew with every dancing molecule in his body.

MILTON "MESS" MEZZROW, *Really the Blues*

It is lucky that the greatest of all jazz musicians is one of those best recorded so that we can follow his music through his recordings from 1923 to the present. A detailed study of Louis Armstrong's style and of his evolution can easily be made by a chronological survey of his recordings.

The oldest Louis Armstrong discs are those which were recorded in 1923 with King Oliver's Creole Jazz Band. With few exceptions Louis is heard only in the ensembles, playing a second trumpet part to King Oliver's lead, although his power and swing contribute largely to the exceptional beauty of these records. There are solos by Louis in *Chimes Blues, Tears,* and *Froggie Moore.*

Chimes Blues is his first recorded solo. The tune is a typical twelve-bar blues played in medium tempo. Louis plays two choruses (twenty-four bars) built on a familiar King Oliver riff which later, slightly altered, became the theme of the well-known *In the Mood*. If the main idea came from King Oliver, the flashy and alert way in which it is played is already very characteristic of Louis. While listening to this solo one notices that by 1923 Louis was already a master of his instrument.

The soloing in *Tears* is a succession of breaks during which the entire band stops playing, except for a few punctuations here and there, which gives one the chance to hear Louis better. The recording is also clearer. Here Louis expresses his own ideas for the first time. This solo is proof that his own style was already shaped at the time.

The next recordings by Louis are those made in New York in 1924 and 1925 with the Fletcher Henderson orchestra. These recordings are valuable only for Louis Armstrong, because the band most of the time used commercial arrangements that sound rather dated, which explains why Fletcher was sometimes called "the Paul Whiteman of the race." It was only in 1926 that Fletcher Henderson began to cut good jazz records. When Louis Armstrong was in the band the only song which was almost successful all the way through was *The Meanest Kind of Blues* (the Columbia version recorded October 24, 1924, not the Vocalion version). Louis is in the limelight for more than half the performance, alternating between or playing with some good clarinet trios.

In other Henderson recordings Louis sometimes takes beautiful solos but only half choruses (sixteen bars usually) and seldom a whole thirty-two-bar chorus. These solos shine like a solitary star in the sky at night. The other soloists sound very poor in comparison to Louis. Their playing sounds corny while that of Louis is just as modern as any solo in any of the later jazz periods.

This is very significant, because Fletcher Henderson's band included at the time musicians who were to become big jazz stars, such as Coleman Hawkins, the greatest of all tenor saxophone players. One has to hear these records to realize the extent to which Louis was the forerunner and how much he influenced the whole of jazz music. Think about it: in 1924 Louis was almost the only musician to represent jazz in its maturity, while most of the other musicians were trying to find their way in a music that was still in its infancy. Within a few years following the entrance of this extraordinary man, the whole of jazz music was transfigured and everyone was playing in the Armstrong style.

When one knows those Henderson records, one is better equipped to understand the impact made by Louis Armstrong in 1924 upon New York musicians. Coleman Hawkins was so deeply moved by Louis' playing during his stay with Louis in Fletcher's band that it made the greatest impression upon him, which remained for the whole of his musical life. Here is how he expressed this in an interview in *Esquire* (August, 1944):

> It happened a long, long time ago. Around 1925, at the Roseland on Broadway. Fletcher Henderson's band was playing and there were thousands of dancers, all yelling and clapping . . . what an orgy of music. The musicians were like demons. The high spot came when Louis Armstrong began *Shanghai Shuffle*. I think they made him play ten choruses. After that piece a dancer lifted Armstrong up onto his shoulders. Fletcher Henderson kept on beating out the rhythm on his piano and I stood silent, feeling almost bashful, asking myself if I would ever be able to attain a small part of Louis Armstrong's greatness. . . .

The best of Louis's solos recorded with Fletcher Henderson are the following: *One of These Days* (one chorus, thirty-two bars); *When You Do What You Do* (one chorus, thirty-two bars); *Everybody Loves My Baby* (Imperial or Regal version, three-quarters of a chorus, twenty-four bars); *Shanghai Shuffle* (Vocalion version, one chorus, thirty-two bars); *Go 'Long Mule* (half chorus, sixteen bars); *Manda* (half chorus, sixteen bars); *Words* (half chorus, sixteen bars); *Copenhagen* (one chorus, thirty-two bars); and *Sugar Foot Stomp* (three choruses, thirty-six bars). In these solos Louis has the fire and fervor of youth but his playing is already full of majestic serenity and great variety. His *Shanghai Shuffle* chorus is built mostly on the repetition of a couple of notes, while in such performances as *Mandy, Make Up Your Mind, One of These Days,* and *Manda,* Louis uses the tune to create melodious phrases that sing as much as they swing. Even in those early days Louis stood apart from the other horn men by the accent of his playing, sometimes dramatic, at other times joyful, with a very pronounced vibrato that gave a poignancy to each note he held, whether long or short.

During his first stay in New York Louis also made a number of recordings for the Okeh Company with the Clarence Williams Blue Five, a group organized only for the recording of the discs.

The performances by the Clarence Williams Blue Five are more valuable than those of Fletcher Henderson. In Sidney Bechet (or Buster Baily on some numbers) Louis had an ideal partner. Buddy Christian was a solid banjoist and Charlie Irvis a good trombone for ensemble playing. Clarence Williams, of course, was not a great pianist, but he does not take any solos on these recordings, which are, next to King Oliver's, the best series of early jazz discs.

It is here for the first time that we hear Louis leading collective improvisations in the flourishing New Orleans style. Although recorded during the same period as those of Fletcher Henderson mentioned above, the Clarence Williams discs show Louis in a very different light. Here we hear Louis not so much as a soloist but as lead man. Louis does not get too far away from the melody but stays close to it, modifying the timing of the notes by rhythmic suspensions (such as the frequent use of rubato) which make his playing swing the most. One has to hear the way he states the melody on the verse of *Everybody Loves My Baby* or *Of All the Wrongs You Done to Me* to measure how his strong personality imposes itself both in the simplest phrases and in the most complex.

Although these records are mostly made up of improvised ensembles, Louis is sometimes featured as a soloist. This is what happens in *Everybody Loves My Baby* where, using a plunger mute, he plays the whole of the last chorus with terrific drive. It is an amazingly powerful solo based firmly upon the beat, during which Louis does not use too many notes, but those he does use he uses in such a way that they constitute the most perfectly constructed solo that one could wish to hear. This is the famous chorus that seized all Harlem and changed the style of innumerable trumpet players. Louis also plays a wonderful solo on *Texas Moaner Blues.*

The best recordings by the Clarence Williams Blue Five with Louis Armstrong are: *Everybody Loves My Baby, Of All the Wrongs You Done to Me, Texas Moaner Blues, I'm a Little Blackbird Looking for a Bluebird,* and *Mandy, Make Up Your Mind.* The last is a little less satisfying because Bechet mostly uses an obnoxious instrument called the sarusophone. Louis softly improvises behind it with such feeling and swing that the listener, at first shocked by the abominable noise produced by the sarusophone, finds a very welcome refuge in this lovely trumpet background. In the other numbers Bechet (or Buster Bailey in the first two mentioned) on the soprano saxophone improvises ravishing arabesques in counterpoint to the trumpet lead, showing a perfect sense of ensemble work. The trombone part complements the other two instruments very well. Thanks to the good recording quality of the Okeh Company, well in advance of all the others, these ensembles still sound very pleasant today.

Another pick-up group of the same kind also recorded for Gennett, but under the name of Red Onion Jazz Babies. These performances are about equal to those on the Okeh label (although less well recorded) and one of them, *Terrible Blues*, is among the best of the old records by Louis.

Besides his discs with Fletcher Henderson and Clarence Williams, Louis also recorded a lot as an accompanist to various blues singers during his first stay in New York.

The most important series is the one recorded for Columbia with Bessie Smith, the greatest of all blues singers. It includes nine performances, five of which, *St. Louis Blues, Cold in Hand Blues, Sobbin' Hearted Blues, Reckless Blues,* and *You've Been a Good Ole Wagon,* rank among the most beautiful blues ever recorded.

Louis Armstrong's cornet accompaniment (he was using a cornet then and continued to do so up until 1926) blends perfectly with Bessie Smith's moving singing. In fact, here Louis is not a mere accompanist. By the phrases which he improvises he answers each vocal phrase and the cornet part can be heard as distinctly as Bessie Smith's singing.

In *Reckless Blues, Cold in Hand Blues,* and *You've Been a Good Ole Wagon,* Louis uses a wa-wa mute, something that he seldom did. In *Reckless Blues* especially he uses it very effectively, with plaintive accents, calls, and exclamations that sound like a human voice in a most adequate reply to Bessie's words.

The *St. Louis Blues* is probably the most authentic version ever recorded of this famous number. There is little doubt that this slow, low-down, and poignant performance interprets the classic Handy blues in the way they were sung and played in the early days.

Perhaps *Sobbin' Hearted Blues* is the most beautiful blues Louis recorded with Bessie Smith. Right from the beginning, when Louis plays the introduction, which consists of the last bars of the chorus followed by the first bars of the verse, the cornet part is extremely melodious and the improvised breaks in answer to Bessie Smith's phrases maintain that "singing" feeling throughout with striking melodic invention. The break before the last vocal phrase even predates some of the things Coleman Hawkins was to play fourteen years later in his masterpiece *Body and Soul*. There is nothing desperate in Louis' accent here, but a soothing beauty like the sight of a rainbow after a storm.

In the first half of *Cold in Hand Blues* Louis' playing has this same accent but the use of the wa-wa changes slightly the mood of the interpretation.

These recordings alone are enough to prove that Louis Armstrong is a perfect blues player. While listening to these performances one can feel that in his childhood Louis was immersed in the blues. But he developed very original ideas when improvising on the traditional twelve-bar blues pattern. If most of the phrases which he played on these recordings sound rather familiar today, let us not forget that innumerable jazz musicians have borrowed the melodic lines Louis Armstrong used on the blues. What no one has been able to equal is the way Louis performs these phrases, that thick, heavy, fleshy, lazy sound which gives Louis' cornet that intense "blue" expression, and which echoes perfectly Bessie Smith's singing. In four other numbers with Bessie Smith—*Nashville Woman's Blues, Careless Love, J. C. Holmes Blues,* and *I Ain't Goin' to Play No Second Fiddle*—a trombone player, Charlie Green, shares the accompaniment with Louis, who consequently is not featured as much as on the previous titles.

During the same period Louis made some records with other blues singers, mainly Ma Rainey and Clara Smith (the two best), Maggie Jones, Coot Grant, and Eva Taylor (Clarence Williams' wife).

The three superb but poorly recorded blues in which Louis and a part of the Fletcher Henderson band accompany Ma Rainey are *See See Rider, Jelly Bean Blues,* and *Countin' the Blues.* The cornet answers soberly and steadily the majestic if not "religious" (Louis' word) singing of Ma Rainey.

In his two last records with Clara Smith, Louis' inspiration is also at its greatest. *Shipwrecked Blues* in a minor key gives Louis a chance to show his dramatic sensitivity. It is regrettable that the cornet was not recorded fully enough, although one is able to hear every note that is played. The cornet part emerges best in *Court House Blues* where Louis displays many pretty ideas.

Of the six sides recorded by Louis with Maggie Jones, *Poor House* does not have much to recommend it. *Thunderstorm Blues, Anybody Here Want to Try My Cabbage,* and *If I Lose Let Me Lose* contain beautiful breaks and short solos by Louis, but the two very best performances by far are *Screamin' the Blues* and *Good Time Flat Blues.* Louis is featured more than in other Maggie Jones records and is just as inspired here as in those with Bessie Smith. He plays in a more exuberant way; his phrases go up and down the horn in response to the voice of Maggie Jones. Here he seems to play for himself, allowing everything that's going through his mind to be brought out in his music, contrary to what happened with Bessie Smith, with whom he carefully followed the words of the singer.

With half of Fletcher Henderson's band Louis also recorded (for Paramount) as accompanist to Coot Grant and Kid Wilson, a popular vaudeville team. While Coot Grant and Kid Wilson engaged in cutting repartee, Louis and the other musicians create a background music of ravishing emotion. One of these performances, *Come on Coot Do That Thing,* is, despite the weakness of the recording, a small masterpiece. The tune is very good typical jazz and Louis swings it so much that one really feels like dancing to it. The band plays one whole chorus alone in which Buster Bailey on clarinet proves an ideal partner for Louis. Among other numbers recorded with Coot and Kid, *Have Your Chill, I'll Be There When Your Fever Rises,* is also a fine tune which Louis beautifully and softly states in the background.

One other record must be mentioned: *Pickin' On Your Baby,* sung by Eva Taylor with the Clarence Williams Blue Five. During all of the last chorus Louis plays an overwhelming solo (not strictly a solo, for the soprano saxophone and trombone back him up) built around two high notes to which he continually returns, holding some of them with an impetuous vibrato. This chorus is entirely different from all the others played by Louis in this period's records. It comes very close to the high-register solos that Louis was to play ten or twelve years later. Here Louis does not look so much for melodic variety or richness. He concentrates on a few notes with such power and expression that he leaves the listener breathless with emotion.

After the New York recordings in 1924 and 1925 came the beginning of the Chicago recording period (from the end of 1925 to the end of 1928), one of the best and certainly the most famous in the whole musical career of Louis Armstrong.

Soon after his return to Chicago the Okeh Company signed him exclusively to their label. This was the beginning of an admirable series by Louis Armstrong's Hot Five. For the first time the name of Louis Armstrong appeared on the record label as a band leader.*

Louis Armstrong's Hot Five was not a regular band but a group formed only to make records. Louis' partners were Johnny Dodds on clarinet, Kid Ory on trombone, John St. Cyr on banjo, and Lil Armstrong, his second wife, on piano. Like the Clarence Williams Blue Five, it was a pure New Orleans-style band (and a first-class one at that), collective improvisations alternating with solos. The few piano solos are the only weak points of these records, but that is rather unimportant in comparison to the other wonderful music. Dodds, Ory and St. Cyr were exactly the type of musicians suited to play with Louis. Although there are no drums or bass (instruments which could not be recorded well at the time) there is a swinging rhythm background, John St. Cyr feeding the musicians wonderfully with his accurate chording and his strong pulse-beat. Along with Louis, St. Cyr is perhaps the trump card in the success of these performances, which, with the records by King Oliver's Creole Jazz Band, are the most beautiful and purest examples of New Orleans style that have been preserved on disc.

The first recording session of the Hot Five took place on

*Most of these recordings have been reissued under the Columbia label.

November 13, 1925. It gave us three fine performances: *My Heart, Yes I'm in the Barrel,* and *Gut Bucket Blues,* the last of which remains in the memories of musicians as one of Louis' masterpieces. It is the blues taken at an easy medium tempo. An excellent introduction by John St. Cyr leads into two perfectly balanced ensemble choruses, a model of good collective improvisations. The solo choruses that follow are by Lil, Ory, Dodds and Louis, who gets a trombone-like sound in a comparatively low register of the cornet. The performance closes with an ensemble chorus, the best of all, in which a combined riff by Louis and Ory makes the music swing so much as to put the most exacting dancers into ecstasy.

It is on *Gut Bucket Blues* that Louis' voice is heard for the first time at length on a record. He does not sing but calls the names of his musicians, stimulating them with a few words such as black musicians like to use during performances. Almost as soon as the banjo begins to play, Louis' voice brings warmth to the music with such words as "Oh, play that thing, Mr. St. Cyr. Lawd, you know you can do it. Everybody from New Orleans can really do that thing, hey, hey!" Similar exhortations are shouted later to other musicians.

The Hot Five next recorded *Come Back Sweet Papa.* Then on February 26, 1926, the group produced one of the most sensational sessions: *Heebie Jeebies, Muskrat Ramble, Cornet Shop Suey, Georgia Grind, You're Next* and *Oriental Strut.*

This was the first time Louis really sang on records. Some start! His two vocal choruses on *Heebie Jeebies,* one with lyrics, the other in "vocalese" (scat singing), disclosed that the trumpet king was also an unbeatable singer. Louis Armstrong's singing was already full of feeling and swing. He was inspired by *Heebie Jeebies*—a very good tune, composed by Boyd Atkins. According to John St. Cyr (*Bulletin of Hot Club de France,* No. 160), it was Louis Armstrong who, in a few minutes, wrote the lyrics for this number.

When recording *Heebie Jeebies* the recording engineer asked who was going to sing. So Louis said nobody because there were no lyrics to this song. So the engineer insists on singing, because vocals were starting to sell well at that time . . . so Louis sat down and scribbled out some lyrics and did a real nice job and the whole thing came out real good while rehearsing it, and everybody was proud about Louis writing such lovely lyrics in a few minutes. Here they are:

I've got the heebies, I mean the jeebies;
Talk 'bout a dance, the heebie jeebies,
You'll see girls and boys,
Faces lit with joy.
If you don't know it,
You ought to learn it.
Come now and do that dance
They call the heebie jeebies dance.

Muskrat Ramble, a typical New Orleans tune having characteristics of French quadrilles, was so successful that numerous bands began to play it a few years later, and to this very day it is still performed all over the world. However, none of the many recordings of *Muskrat Ramble* can be compared to Louis Armstrong's original version, which is taken at a perfect tempo for the song. Louis plays a solo typical of his style of that period. It is still the classical New Orleans trumpet style with neat, well-cut phrasing, leaning on the beat, but much richer and more inventive than other trumpet styles of that era. This style was emulated by Muggsy Spanier on trumpet and Jimmy Harrison on trombone. The latter even succeeded in putting almost as much melody into his solos as Louis, as well as phrases of exactly the same shape. One has only to listen, for instance, to Jimmy Harrison's trombone solo in Chick Webb's *Heebie Jeebies* and compare it with Louis' solo in *Muskrat Ramble.* It is impossible not to be struck by the similarity of the phrases and accent.

On *Cornet Shop Suey* Louis scores a personal triumph. He plays continuously except for the piano chorus and shows at times his amazing technique in fast phrases in different registers of the cornet. The melody of *Cornet Shop Suey,* verse and chorus, was composed by Louis and is very pretty. The verse is especially full of melody and the way in which Louis states it at the beginning of the record gives it a haunting quality.

Cornet Shop Suey made a terrific impact upon all jazz musicians. Ten years later, when Roy Eldridge began to amaze the jazz world with his virtuosity and power, musicians could not find a better comparison than to say, "Roy Eldridge reminds us of the Louis Armstrong of *Cornet Shop Suey.*" Despite the fact that this beautiful performance has some weak spots—the piano solo is insignificant and the tempo slows down—musicians still talk of it as one of Louis' masterpieces.

Oriental Strut is a number composed by John St. Cyr which has a pretty verse. In it Louis improvises an entire stop-time chorus full of invention, as he was to do in several other Hot Five records.

Georgia Grind is a blues in slow tempo (slow for those days, when slow tempos were good dancing tempos) with four vocal choruses, two by Lil and two by Louis, with the verse in a minor key played poignantly on cornet and a swinging chorus in a major key. A few years later Jack

Teagarden reproduced Louis' solo on the verse, note for note, on trombone in the well-known recording of *Makin' Friends* by Eddie Condon and other Chicagoans.

The three following sessions by the Hot Five also in 1926 did not produce such exceptional performances as the earlier ones, although none of them should be neglected.

The first one included *Don't Forget to Mess Around, I'm Gonna Gitch, Dropping Shucks,* and *Who's It?* The first three have vocal choruses by Louis Armstrong which are unlikely to convert *bel canto* fans to jazz. There is plenty of good jazz most of the time, but *Who's It?* is the weakest of all Hot Five recordings. Ory plays a strange trombone solo and Louis is heard on a curious instrument sometimes used in the old days of jazz, the slide whistle. The short cornet passages are the only great moments in this performance of a number whose first phrase was used years later in the theme of Maurice Chevalier's *On Veut Tant S'Aimer Chérie.*

The next session included *The King of the Zulus* with an impressive cornet chorus full of melodic ideas. *Sweet Little Papa* and *Big Fat Ma and Skinny Pa* are on the whole very good. *Lonesome Blues* is a really slow blues made up of five choruses, three by Johnny Dodds on clarinet and two sung by Louis, the latter being a typical example of blues sung in the New Orleans style.

Next came *Jazz Lips* and *Skid-da-de-dat* in which Louis uses scat singing as suggested by the title. *Sunset Café Stomp* and *Big Butter and Egg Man from the West* could be counted among the Hot Five's masterpieces if they had not been spoiled by Mae Alix's vocal chorus in each loudly recorded piece. Louis reaches the height of inspiration in both the ravishing verse and crazy coda on *Sunset Café,* and the chorus on *Big Butter and Egg Man* is among the most melodious of Louis' inventions. It is this chorus which made the number *Big Butter and Egg Man* as famous among jazz musicians as *Cornet Shop Suey*. Many of them learned it by heart, and it was even harmonized for several instruments and recorded by Wingy Mannone's band.

Up until then the recording of the Hot Five, although acoustical, was of remarkable quality and superior to most recordings of that time. With *Irish Black Bottom* and *You Made Me Love You*, two very good performances, the Hot Five for the first time benefited from electrical recording techniques. Of course, from then on the music sounded all the better for it.

Around the same time the Hot Five recorded two numbers for the Brunswick Company, *Georgia Bo Bo* and *Drop That Sack*, which were released on the Vocalion label under the name of Lil's Hot Shots, because Louis, as an exclusive Okeh artist, was not permitted to record for another label. This practice was not uncommon; musicians would often record for a company other than the one which had signed them exclusively, providing that their names did not appear on the label. However, instead of just playing his trumpet, Louis also sang in one number, *Georgia Bo Bo*, and his voice could be recognized among thousands. It is reported that the president of the Okeh Company called Louis to his office. The record was on the turntable and, without saying a word, the president put the record on and, when the vocal chorus was reached, asked the musician, "Do you know who is singing, Louis?" "I don't know, sir, but I won't do it again," was the reply as Louis disappeared through the door. And that was that.

The rather loud recording of these two numbers makes the ensemble work sound confused, but the music is good. Johnny Dodds plays one of the best solos in *Georgia Bo Bo* and the two blues choruses sung by Louis swing a great deal.

In May, 1927, Louis Armstrong recorded more masterpieces for Okeh. The Hot Five became the Hot Seven with the addition of Peter Briggs on tuba and Baby Dodds on drums. Unfortunately, the latter was only able to use cymbals, for it was not yet possible to record snare or bass drums accurately. There were two other changes. The trombone was no longer Ory but John Thomas instead, and Louis, once and for all, switched from cornet to trumpet, whose more powerful and brilliant tone suited him better.

During the month of May, six recording sessions were made by Louis within eight days. *Willie the Weeper, Wild Man Blues, Alligator Crawl, Potato Head Blues, Melancholy Blues, Weary Blues, Twelfth Street Rag, Keyhole Blues, Gully Low Blues,* and *That's When I'll Come Back to You* are the most beautiful fruits of these sessions. Louis is in top form. He becomes more and more daring: his long solo in *Wild Man Blues* is full of phrases which had never before been heard in jazz. Most unexpected, as they follow one another, they are executed with incredible power that would surely have caused the walls of Jericho to fall. The influence of this *Wild Man Blues* on younger trumpet players has been incalculable. Louis got strong support from his augmented rhythm section.

Three more of these recordings are marvelous. The first, *Willie the Weeper,* opens with a very cohesive, collective improvisation. After some good solos John St. Cyr takes a characteristic New Orleans-style guitar chorus, at the end of which a few swinging chords pave the way for Louis' entrance. Louis then plays a grandiose sixteen-bar solo, attacking each note with terrific strength. Many of the notes are played on the up-beat while Baby Dodds supports them by an incisive cymbal back-beat. At the end of each chorus Louis plays a vibrating call in the high register, and the entire band plays the last chorus with him as Baby Dodds continues to play a swinging cymbal back-beat. This last chorus is one of the greatest collective improvisations ever captured on record. Although all the musicians contribute to the high quality of the performance, it is mostly the perfect combination of Louis' trumpet and Baby Dodds' cymbal that makes it exceptional. Such a phenomenon is not rare in jazz but there are few examples of it on records, because until the invention of the long-playing disc, performances were too short for musicians to have a chance to give out their best.

Potato Head Blues contains collective improvisations almost as perfect as those in *Willie the Weeper*. Louis plays two solos. He states the verse with beautiful embellishments and improvises a stop chorus which is not only an aggregation of the most brilliant breaks, but also shows a very logical development of the excellent idea which starts the solo. This is one of Louis' most famous choruses and hundreds of musicians have borrowed several of the phrases played here and there within it.

Gully Low Blues starts at a fast tempo but soon becomes a low-down, slow blues. Johnny Dodds plays two fine clarinet choruses, one in the high register, the other in the low register, sandwiching two intense vocal choruses by Louis, "Mama, mama, mama, why do you treat me so?" (the English Parlophone edition of this record, instead of *Gully Low Blues*, was entitled *Mama Why Do You Treat Me So?*). A little further on Louis plays a unique trumpet chorus divided into two-bar phrases, each of which begins by one violently attacked and shaken high note. A couple of musicians told me that there Louis was using a King Oliver idea, but it is unlikely that even King Oliver could have played a solo of this kind in such an overwhelming way. In order to make such a chorus sound like that one needs exceptional mastery of the trumpet, a lot of power allied to delicate sensitivity. Many musicians have tried to emulate this solo but no one has succeeded in expressing as much through it as Louis did. A smooth trumpet player like Joe Smith lacked some of the power in the execution of the vibrated high note, as is obvious upon listening to Bessie Smith's *Hard Driving Papa,* where the trumpet breaks are similar to the *Gully Low Blues* solo. Bill Coleman uses it in his recording of *Hang Over Blues* with Alix Combelle. His high notes have more bite than Joe Smith's but lack Louis' weight. One of Count Basie's trumpet players also imitated this solo as an accompaniment to Jimmy Rushing's vocal in Basie's *Blues in the Dark.* Even trombonists attempted this solo, such as Vic Dickenson in *Blues at Blue Note.* But there is always something missing, either power or volume, and thus the solo loses either its dynamic quality or its sensitivity and tends to become crude, losing some of its emotional value. This again proves how accomplished a musician Louis is.

Curiously enough, *Gully Low Blues* was recorded twice within twenty-four hours by the Hot Seven with different lyrics. It was not until fourteen years later that the other version, entitled *S.O.L. Blues,* was issued. Although valuable, this version is not as good as *Gully Low Blues.*

Twelfth Street Rag had the same fate as *S.O.L. Blues.* First recorded in May, 1927, it was not released until 1941, when it appeared under the Columbia label. The Okeh Company probably did not issue it in its day because of some cracked notes in the trumpet chorus. But this is very unimportant because Louis takes an unforgettable chorus which is very original and different from any other that he has recorded. To measure how inspired Louis was on this date one has to be familiar with the theme of *Twelfth Street Rag* and with the way this number is usually played. Instead of the expected fast tempo, Louis takes it at a very moderate tempo which allows him to get things out of this tune that had never before been heard and have not been heard since. There is as much humor as invention in this bewildering juggling with the theme of *Twelfth Street Rag*. Rarely has Louis accumulated so many ideas in just thirty-two bars. Each phrase comes as a surprise. One finds there all the complexities of so-called modern trumpet playing and much more melody.

The five other recordings by the Hot Seven are good too. *That's When I'll Come Back to You* has an imploring vocal by Lil to whom Louis replies with a bold cynicism. *Weary Blues* is full of fire. *Alligator Crawl,* an excellent Fats Waller composition, features Louis in his most melodious vein, firmly supported by Baby Dodds' cymbal and Pete Briggs' tuba. Louis' trumpet solo in *Melancholy Blues* sounds as if he were singing. *Keyhole Blues* is even better because Louis is featured at greater length, in fact, all the way through with the exception of one clarinet chorus. Louis delivers a swinging scat vocal chorus, and his trumpet part in the first half of the last ensemble chorus consists of just a very effective three-note riff, which predates the ensemble riffing big bands were to use during the 1930s.

Between those Hot Seven sessions Louis recorded on May 10, 1927, one number, *Chicago Breakdown,* with Carroll Dickerson's orchestra, the band with which he was regularly playing at the Sunset Café in Chicago. Earl

Hines (piano), Honoré Dutrey (trombone), and Rip Bassett (guitar) were among the members of this band. This side was also not issued until 1941. Although not as outstanding as those by the Hot Seven, the performance contains a magnificent trumpet part.

For the following session, toward the end of 1927, the Hot Seven was reduced to the Hot Five, as previously, and Kid Ory was back in the trombone chair. The numbers recorded were: *Put 'Em Down Blues, Ory's Creole Trombone, The Last Time, Struttin' With Some Barbecue, Got No Blues, Once In a While, I'm Not Rough, Hotter Than That,* and *Savoy Blues.*

Put 'Em Down Blues is one of Louis' prettiest and most original compositions. Its structure (a forty-eight-bar chorus) differs from that of any other number composed by jazz musicians. It is one of the most beautiful performances recorded by the Hot Five. The trumpet solo, as melodious as a Benny Carter chorus (Benny Carter is rightfully considered as just about the most melodious of all jazzmen), really tells a story. Each phrase is the perfect continuation of the previous one, the whole thing forming one of the most coherent and perfectly built solos in the history of jazz.

Ory's Creole Trombone is one of those New Orleans parade-like tunes which gives Kid Ory a chance to play some picturesque trombone breaks. Louis leads the numerous ensembles with a lot of drive, graced here and there with subtle variations. The short trumpet solo includes several cracked notes and that is probably the reason why the recording was not released before 1941, which was also the case with *The Last Time.* It is not easy to understand why the Okeh Company did not release the latter in its time because it is an entirely successful performance.

Struttin' With Some Barbecue and *Once In a While* (not to be confused with another number of the same title which Louis was to record for Decca ten years later) are made up of collective improvisations of exceptional quality. Each number includes a stop chorus by Louis just as great as the one in *Potato Head Blues.* Of all the numbers composed by Louis Armstrong, *Struttin' With Some Barbecue* is the most famous and many bands now have it in their repertoires.*

Got No Blues is not as perfect as some of the other Hot Five productions because the tempo slows down. However, it is a brilliant interpretation nevertheless.

In the three last numbers a wonderful guitarist, Lonnie Johnson, was added to the Hot Five, reinforcing the blues feeling in *I'm Not Rough* by his ensemble playing as well as by his solo, typical of the New Orleans blues style. *I'm Not Rough* is one of the best blues that the Hot Five recorded, the first half consisting of a collective improvisation of rare homogeneity. Louis' trumpet part really reaches here to the very core of the blues.

Savoy Blues is also a blues but of a different kind and performed in a different way. Louis first plays a sixteen-bar theme, then the band goes into the regular twelve-bar blues. There is one chorus of ensemble riffing and one chorus by just two guitars, Lonnie Johnson playing the lead and John St. Cyr the accompaniment. This guitar chorus is preceded by an interlude played by St. Cyr alone and followed by another one played by both guitarists. This is followed by two choruses by Louis, one by Kid Ory,

*Several of Louis' compositions are credited on the label to his second wife, Lil Hardin. Lil might have collaborated in the composition of these numbers, but their style reflects Louis' musical personality so much that there is little doubt that the main theme and ideas originally came from him.

another chorus of ensemble riffing, and one of collective improvisation. Louis' solo, with his sinuous, subtle, ravishing lines, smoothly played, ranks among his greatest and the phrases he plays in the beginning of his second solo-chorus have been quoted by other musicians in many solos. And there is that beautiful note held with admirable vibrato by Louis in the seventeenth bar.

Hotter Than That, an improvisation on the chords of the main strain of *Tiger Rag*, contains two amazing choruses by Louis, one on trumpet with several fast phrases, typical of the Armstrong-inspired style that Earl Hines was using on piano at the time when Louis and he often played together; the other one is an excellent scat vocal followed by a spirited exchange between Louis' voice and Lonnie Johnson's guitar.

In April, 1927, Louis recorded behind Okeh's back and cut eight numbers for the Brunswick Company. Four were issued on the Vocalion label under the names of Jimmy Bertrand's Washboard Wizards: *Easy Come Easy Go Blues, The Blues Stampede, I'm Goin' Huntin',* and *If You Want to Be My Sugar Papa.* It was a four-piece group with Johnny Dodds on clarinet, Jimmy Blythe on piano, and Jimmy Bertrand on Washboard. The four other numbers, *Wild Man Blues, Melancholy, New Orleans Stomp,* and *Weary Blues,* issued under the name of Johnny Dodds' Black Bottom Stompers, were recorded by a seven-piece band including Earl Hines on piano and, of course, Johnny Dodds. This time Louis did not take any chances of being recognized as he had done the year before. Not only did he not take any vocal but went so far as to disguise his trumpet style, playing softer than usual and avoiding the powerful effects that would give him away. It seems that these recordings went unnoticed by the Okeh Company.* Despite Louis' efforts to modify his playing, people well acquainted with his music were able to recognize him, especially on *Wild Man Blues*. I must confess, however, that I was at first fooled by two of the numbers, *Weary Blues* and *New Orleans Stomp*.

In 1928, Louis Armstrong's Hot Five continued to record for Okeh, but he had entirely changed the little group. The new Hot Five now included Earl Hines on piano, Zutty Singleton on drums, Mancy Cara on banjo, Fred Robinson on trombone, and Jimmy Strong on both clarinet and tenor saxophone. Six numbers, *Fireworks, Skip the Gutter, A Monday Date, West End Blues, Sugar Foot Strut*, and *Don't Jive Me* were recorded in June (the last title was released only in 1941), and a few weeks later three others were waxed: *Two Deuces, Squeeze Me*, and *Knee Drops*.

This new Hot Five was about equal to the previous one. Of course, Jimmy Strong is far from being a Johnny Dodds, and his acid tone is sometimes harsh on the listener's ear; and Fred Robinson is not a Kid Ory, although he is a fairly good man for ensemble playing and for the blues. The disappearance of St. Cyr is more than compensated for by the inclusion of Earl Hines, one of the greatest jazz soloists ever. Mancy Cara is a good banjoist with a solid tempo. Unfortunately, Zutty, like Baby Dodds the year before, could use neither the snare nor the bass drum and had to play only cymbals or the like. It was on hand-cymbals that he performed the exciting little solos in *Fireworks, Sugar Foot Strut*, and *A Monday Date*.

The spirit of the music is the same as the old Hot Five

*Years later they were reissued under the name of Louis Armstrong, who was no longer under exclusive contract to the Okeh Company, which no longer existed, having been bought out by Columbia.

and the performances have the same shape: collective improvisations in the traditional New Orleans style at the beginning and the end, with solos in the middle. Because of the importance of the clarinet in this type of performance, the front line was better in the first Hot Five; but with Earl on piano instead of Lil, the level of the solos is much higher.

Without any doubt, the masterpiece of this new series is *West End Blues* which has often been quoted by many people as their favorite Louis Armstrong recording. Never has a blues been so loudly recorded. It opens with a formidable trumpet introduction with no accompaniment, which left all musicians speechless. During the introduction Louis goes up and down his horn with rapid and beautiful phrases, sounding a mysterious kind of call. The last note in a low register brings in the first ensemble chorus, slow, heavy, saturated with the blues atmosphere, a chorus which ends by an ascension which is like an echo of the introduction. Fred Robinson then states the second strain of *West End Blues* on trombone in a lazy way. The following chorus is a duet between Jimmy Strong in the low register of the clarinet and Louis, who answers by improvising beautiful and nostalgic scat breaks. His voice here is especially tender and suave. Earl Hines follows with a piano chorus which corresponds closely to Louis' vocal style. Then there is the last chorus, beginning with three powerfully attacked trumpet notes. The third one is held in the high register for several bars, giving way to a very effective repetition of several notes in the same register, and the chorus ends with a short piano part before a few lazy trumpet notes from Louis in the low register conclude the performance.

Next to *West End Blues, Skip the Gutter* is probably the most beautiful performance in this series of recordings. It gives evidence of the musical friendship between Louis and Earl, who improvise a grandiose duet thirty-two bars long. No sooner does one finish a phrase than the other improvises another one which is a perfect continuation. The melodic style of these two giants of jazz is so alike that one has the impression the phrases come out of the same mind. Of all the musicians who come really close to Louis' style, Earl has been the closest. There is a shorter duet toward the end of *Skip the Gutter* of a different kind, when Earl Hines hits a chord and Louis improvises a break on it, repeating this three times.

Fireworks, Knee Drops, and *A Monday Date* are taken at fast tempos. *Knee Drops* is another improvisation on the chords of *Tiger Rag. A Monday Date* is an Earl Hines' tune. It contains, like *Sugar Foot Strut,* a vocal chorus by Louis accompanied by the piano in such an original and audacious way that one has to marvel at the understanding between these two musicians. *A Monday Date* also has a muted trumpet chorus of rare lyrical invention. In *Squeeze Me* there is another of those exuberant scat choruses by Louis against a vocal background hummed by a couple of his musicians.

In December, 1928, Louis recorded with his Hot Five an unforgettable series of interpretations: *No Papa No, Basin Street Blues, No One Else but You, Beau Koo Jack, Save It Pretty Mama, Muggles, St. James Infirmary, Heah Me Talkin' to Ya,* and *Tight Like This.*

The Hot Five became in fact the Hot Six for most of these recordings with the addition of Don Redman on alto saxophone and clarinet. The ensembles are not all improvised but sometimes arranged in a straightforward way by Don Redman. These nice little arrangements are often more effective than the collective improvisations of the previous discs in which Jimmy Strong was not a good enough clarinetist to play with Louis Armstrong.

However, it is not the addition of Don Redman and his arrangements that brings the biggest change in this new series. It is Zutty's full set of drums recorded for the first time. Instead of a very incomplete rhythm section as in the previous recordings, we can now hear Zutty's pedal on the bass drums (as well as his wire brushes on the snare), and hear it very well, because seldom have the four beats on the bass drum been so well recorded. It is fortunate because few drummers succeed in getting such a vibrant sound from the bass drum. It is powerful yet never heavy, and people who think it is too heavy have become too accustomed to the effeminate playing of so many contemporary drummers. Zutty's drumming wonderfully emphasizes the quality of Louis, Earl and the other musicians' work, and one can feel that they are all inspired by the terrific drumming behind them. Zutty's style is the ideal one for Louis and Earl, because it has exactly the same pulse and feeling. Some years later, after having played with various great drummers, Louis Armstrong was reported to have said, "Ain't nobody to back me up like my pal Zutty." The getting together of these three jazz giants—Louis, Earl and Zutty—explains the unique quality of these records. Bearing in mind that Louis and Earl have never played better and seldom been recorded better, it is easy to understand why these performances are among the best which have been preserved on disc. All the virtues of the best jazz are presented here and at their highest level. The engineers of the Okeh company might never have realized how proud they were entitled to be of their work. Despite the many developments in recording techniques, up until now no one has succeeded in getting a more perfect orchestral balance, at least in the domain of jazz.

The first two performances of this series, *No, Papa, No*, which was originally issued under the title *No*, and *Basin Street Blues* were recorded without Don Redman. *No, Papa, No* is a twelve-bar blues taken in semi-slow tempo. After an ensemble introduction Louis plays a beautiful chorus with amazing support from Earl Hines, which is a counterpoint rather than an accompaniment. Further on Earl plays one of his finest solos on the blues and Fred Robinson surpasses himself on trombone.

Louis Armstrong considers *Basin Street Blues* as one of his best records and he has every reason to do so. A very simple head arrangement gives the music a form and color all its own. Earl Hines plays the introduction and first chorus on celeste with a background of "organ chords" by the band. Louis then goes into the twelve-bar blues for just one chorus. It is a model chorus on the blues and many trumpet players have used this type of phrasing, for instance, Cootie Williams on Duke Ellington's recording of *Saratoga Swing*. A piano interlude by Earl Hines leads into a scat chorus by Louis with a background hummed by other musicians. After another piano interlude the power that has been held back since the beginning suddenly bursts forth with a grandiose trumpet chorus and wide-moving phrases surge out, contrasting with fantastic romping in the high register. In the last chorus Louis' trumpet shouts on for a while, then sort of progressively dims down along with the band, to the *demi-teinte* of the beginning, and the performance ends as it began with Earl Hines at the celeste.

Thank goodness that this version of *Basin Street Blues* was recorded before Glenn Miller and Jack Teagarden added a verse, "Aint you glad you came with me to the Mississippi?" which was heard for the first time in 1931.

The next session with Don Redman gave us the recording of *No One Else But You, Save It Pretty Mama*, and *Beau Koo Jack*. The last tune, composed and arranged by Alex Hill, contains an impetuous trumpet chorus with Zutty playing only the strong beats on the bass drums instead of his usual four beats, in order to conform to this type of number.

No One Else But You, taken in a fine medium tempo, is one of the greatest recordings of 1928. The ensembles at the beginning and end have been very well arranged by Don Redman. It is in this number that the rhythm section is heard the best, with Earl Hines, Zutty, and Mancy Cara playing as one. The four beats played all the way through by Zutty on the bass drum give a wonderful lift to the performance. Here one cannot help but feel that the drums, when well played, are the heart of the jazz orchestra.

Louis takes two choruses. In the first one, beautifully conceived, he displays bewildering invention, and Earl Hines follows the trumpet lines step by step with amazing intuition, feeding Louis with chords and punctuations that fall right in with Louis' ideas. Then, when Louis sings the next chorus, Earl improvises some of his dazzling piano fireworks which again provide a perfect background to the beautiful vocal.

There is no arrangement on *Save It Pretty Mama* and it seems that Jimmy Strong did not play on this one. The first chorus is by Louis on muted trumpet against Don Redman's smooth subtone clarinet. Earl Hines' inventiveness is shown to good advantage during the second chorus with the most valuable and unexpected phrases. The third chorus is an alto saxophone solo in a charming melodic vein, played with perfect relaxation by Don Redman, and is one of the best he recorded. Louis sings the fourth chorus in a moving way, prettily backed by Earl

Hines as usual. The last chorus is a good collective improvisation with Don Redman on clarinet.

Muggles, recorded without Don Redman, is a twelve-bar blues, opening in slow tempo with a piano chorus strongly supported by Zutty. The next two choruses, by Fred Robinson and Jimmy Strong, are not up to the same level, but then, all of a sudden, Louis introduces a faster tempo and plays one of the most swinging choruses that one could wish to hear, with a fascinating repetition, insisting on one note for most of the chorus. During the last bars everyone returns to the slow tempo and Louis starts the final chorus with one of King Oliver's favorite riffs, while Earl Hines' right hand creates an exciting counterpart.

Louis and Earl alone recorded *Weather Bird.* It has sometimes been considered a trumpet solo. In fact it is a trumpet/piano duet, throughout which these two jazz giants exchange musical ideas, each one stimulating the other with the most audacious and unexpected discoveries. This is one of the craziest and best improvisations ever put on record. *Weather Bird* is none other than the ragtime recorded five years earlier by Louis with King Oliver's band under the title of *Weather Bird Rag,* but the way Louis and Earl interpret it gives it an entirely new dimension. Just a small remark: two interludes were planned (the only non-improvised spots in the record) but Earl forgot one. Earl goes into the chorus while Louis starts playing the interlude, so Earl immediately goes back to the interlude.

The last session of this December, 1928, series which was also to be the last by the Hot Five, saw the recording of *Heah' Me Talkin' to Ya, St. James Infirmary,* and *Tight Like This.*

Heah' Me Talkin' to Ya is the same type of interpretation as *No One Else But You.* Chorus and verse are first stated by the whole band and both are arranged by Don Redman. There are three solo choruses, one by Earl Hines, one by Don Redman on alto saxophone (again one of his best), and the third and last by Louis on trumpet whose first phrase, which starts on the last beats of the preceding chorus, is almost five bars long and shows the King of Jazz at his greatest. With the exception of three vocal choruses and a short piano solo, *St. James Infirmary* consists of ensembles arranged in a simple but effective way by Don Redman. The statement of this tune in a minor key introduces, right from the start, a dramatic atmosphere which dominates the whole record, largely due to the somber accent of Louis Armstrong's trumpet. The summit of the interpretation is the long vocal by Louis, one of his most poignant (his voice sumptuously recorded). With the help of Zutty's wire brushes on the snare drums and Earl Hines' piano accompaniment, Louis swings more than words can express.

Tight Like This, also in a minor key, has the same type of dramatic accent as *St. James Infirmary.* After the warm statement of the tune by all the musicians, Earl Hines' pungent piano improvisation is taken up by Louis to the end of the disc. These three trumpet choruses form one of the most overwhelming solos that he has ever recorded. When he begins, it sounds like a keen, eager, insistent call played in the low register; then phrases start moving in a more elaborate way, up and down the horn until that one desperate long note, which Louis holds high, and on which he keeps insisting during the last phrases. All the hardships of being a man seem to be expressed in this solo.

This, the last session by the Hot Five, was also the end of what could be called Louis Armstrong's great Chicago period.

22. Edmund Hall and Louis Armstrong.

23. Louis at home with his NARAS (National Academy of Recording Arts and Sciences) trophy, circa 1966.

24. Louis and the All Stars, Steel Pier, Atlantic City, circa 1965. Buddy Catlett (bass), Danny Barcelona (drums), Buster Bailey (clarinet), Louis, Tyree Glenn (trombone), Billy Kyle (piano).

25. Louis and All Stars rehearsing for "Mardi Gras" Show, Jones Beach, Long Island, New York. Marty Napoleon, Tyree Glenn, Danny Barcelona, Louis, Buddy Catlett (partially hidden), and Buster Bailey.

26. Louis on the back porch of his Corona, Long Island home, circa 1966.

27. Louis at home, Corona, Long Island, 1966.

28. Louis with his wife Lucille; trumpeter Joe Thomas; Joe's wife, singer Babe Mathews; and song publisher-promoter Harrison Smith.

29. Louis and his trombonist Tyree Glenn, 1967.

Before going any further, mention should be made of numerous other recordings made by Louis Armstrong in Chicago between 1925 and 1929—two with a band and all the others with various blues singers—records which were not dealt with until now in order not to interrupt the story of the Hot Five sessions.

The two interpretations with a band, *Stomp Off, Let's Go* and *Statis Strut,* were recorded in 1926 by Erskine Tate's orchestra, of which Louis was then a member. Louis takes brilliant trumpet solos, especially on *Static Strut,* in which he is "real gone" as the musicians used to say. This number also has good piano solos by Teddy Weatherford.

Louis recorded about fifty numbers, all for Okeh, as an accompanist, most of the time with just a pianist, sometimes with other musicians. He can be heard in records by Hociel Thomas, Bertha "Chippie" Hill, Baby Mack, Sippie Wallace, Nolan Welsh, Lillie Delk Christian—not one of them outstanding singers, to say the least. So it is because of Louis himself that these recordings are worth being preserved, at least when Louis has an important role, which is often the case. Very few are the interpretations in which Louis does not reach his best level of inspiration, as on *Jack O'Diamond Blues* and *Special Delivery Mail* by Sippie Wallace.

I have not been able to hear all of these records, as some were unavailable even before I was aware of their existence, and up to now they have not been reissued. However, I know the majority of them, among which six numbers stand out because Louis is well featured all the way through: *Low Land Blues, Kid Man Blues, Pleadin' For the Blues, Pratt City Blues* with Bertha "Chippie" Hill, *St. Peter Blues* and *The Bridwell Blues* with Nolan Welsh. The breaks improvised by Louis between the vocal phrases sound more beautiful each time and are full of invention and emotion. Besides, each of these six interpretations contains a solo chorus by Louis. It is worth mentioning that the cornet Louis was still using is exceptionally well recorded in *Pratt City Blues* and *Pleadin' For the Blues*.

The most curious session in which Louis participated is, without doubt, the one with Lillie Delk Christian in December, 1928, the same week he made the last and most beautiful Hot Five recording. Lillie Delk Christian is indeed a poor singer. She has no swing, lacks feeling for phrasing, and has a piercing nasal voice which overloud recording succeeded in making almost unbearable. Despite this, the four numbers made at this session, *I Must Have That Man, Baby, Sweethearts On Parade,* and *I Can't Give You Anything But Love,* are worth saving from complete oblivion because never was a singer blessed with such marvelous accompaniment. Louis is helped by Jimmie Noone on clarinet, Earl Hines on piano, and Mancy Cara on guitar. These are the only recordings which Louis, Earl, and Jimmie, three jazz giants just made for each other, recorded together. It is obvious that all three are at their best. There are other records on which each played as well as they do here, but none on which they played better.

In *I Can't Give You Anything But Love,* which was recorded at the beginning of the session when the musicians were still warming up, they play with much feeling. But it is with *Baby,* recorded next, that Louis, Earl, and Jimmie are completely "gone." Behind the silly singing of Lillie Delk Christian, which one might succeed in overlooking if the recording were not so loud, the four musicians immediately create music full of warmth and tension. When Lillie Delk has finished the verse and chorus, an instrumental chorus by the quartet is heard in which Jimmie Noone's clarinet part mixes with Louis' trumpet even better than Johnny Dodds' did in the Hot Five, and even better than Sidney Bechet's soprano saxophone in the old Clarence Williams Blue Five. What a pity that Jimmie Noone recorded so little with Louis Armstrong!

In the two other numbers, *I Must Have That Man* and *Sweethearts On Parade,* the music is even more inspired, if this is possible. In each number the quartet plays a half-chorus without the singer. Right from his first notes Louis bursts out with tense phrases every time. Jimmie Noone's clarinet counterpoint is so musical that it is a wonder how he creates a beautiful melodic line of his own and follows and blends in with the trumpet part at the same time. The brief union of Louis Armstrong and Jimmie Noone on that date must stay as one of the high peaks of jazz music on record.

At the beginning of *I Must Have That Man,* there is a beautiful trumpet introduction. Earl Hines, with his piano introduction on *Sweethearts On Parade,* establishes a solid and masterful tempo which contributes a lot to the quality of the interpretation. Mancy Cara's firm and swinging guitar gives an excellent rhythmic and harmonic backing. So, all the way through, while Lillie Delk imperturbably pushes on with her squeaky vocals, one can enjoy Louis', Earl's, and Jimmie's beautiful improvisations, for what they play can be heard distinctly. Yet never was there such an awkward association in the entire history of jazz, a vocalist coming from nowhere, for no reason accompanied by great instrumentalists who not only do not seem to mind the vocal but play melodious, swinging, and moving music, a music heard on only a few records. Yes, December, 1928, was a grand month in

Louis Armstrong's recording calendar.

Louis had already backed Lillie Delk Christian a year before on four numbers with Earl Hines, Jimmie Noone, and a guitarist who, it seems, was John St. Cyr. But, although the accompaniment and the half-choruses by the quartet are full of good things, it is not comparable to the exceptional inspiration of the other session. Let me mention that at the end of *Too Busy* Louis seems to delight in improvising alongside Lillie Delk's singing, and the contrast between the voice and style of the two singers is astounding.

Soon after his arrival in New York, Louis Armstrong took part in two recording sessions as an accompanist during June and July of 1929. One was with the syrupy singer, Seger Ellis, and the Dorsey Brothers (Jimmy on clarinet and Tommy on trombone) in which Louis' trumpet is heard very little except when he solos on *To Be in Love* and *S'posin*. The other session was with Victoria Spivey, a good blues singer. Here the accompaniment is much more interesting because Louis is helped by what used to be his Hot Five, with the exception of Earl Hines, who was replaced by Gene Anderson, the pianist in Carroll Dickerson's band. Louis plays beautifully, as does Zutty on drums. These were the two last sessions which Louis made as an accompanist, and it is the last time that he recorded without his name being on the label. From then on Louis would become too big a star for the record companies not to use his name on records.

And then came the beginning in New York of a new series of orchestral recordings by Louis. First, when Louis arrived in town, in March, 1929, four numbers were made: *Mahogany Hall Stomp, I Can't Give You Anything But Love, Knocking a Jug,* and *I'm Gonna Stomp Mr. Henry Lee,* which was never issued.

Although recorded the same day, these four interpretations did not feature the same musicians. In the last two Louis was surrounded by a mixed band (i.e. composed of both black and white musicians): Jack Teagarden on trombone, Joe Sullivan on piano, Eddie Lang on guitar, Happy Cauldwell on tenor saxophone, and Kaiser Marshall on drums. *Knocking a Jug* is nothing but a sequence of solos on the twelve-bar blues. Out of seven choruses Louis plays only the last two. One is waiting for him during almost all of the record and, as the other solos are not exceptional, the wait seems long. Despite the two choruses by Louis, just as marvelous as his others of the same period, *Knocking a Jug* does not compare with the Hot Five recordings. Besides, Kaiser Marshall, who is prominently recorded and usually an excellent drummer, lacks a feeling of relaxation here. Toward the beginning of Louis' second chorus he rushes the tempo in a surprising way for a matter of seconds.

The two other numbers were recorded with Luis Russell's band, minus his trumpet player and guitarist, the latter being replaced by Eddie Condon on banjo in *I Can't Give You Anything But Love,* and by Lonnie Johnson on guitar in *Mahogany Hall Stomp.* These two interpretations are vastly superior to *Knocking a Jug* because Louis can be heard almost all the way through and the rhythm section with the great Pops Foster on bass swings much more.

I Can't Give You Anything But Love is one of Louis Armstrong's most celebrated recordings. Except for the second half of the first chorus played by Higginbotham on trombone, Louis solos all the time, while in the background the saxophone section softly states the theme. This uninterrupted statement of the theme behind the trumpet and vocal gives one a chance to realize easily the richness of Louis' invention in his variations as when, for instance, his attack on some of his phrases is held back as late as possible, thus creating a strong tension. Louis plays the first half of the first chorus with a mute, sings the whole of the second, and without mute plays with terrific power in the third, ending by a progressive ascension up to high F. Both the trumpet and vocal choruses have been copied many times. The great singer Ethel Waters in her recording of *I Can't Give You Anything But Love* reproduced almost note for note Louis' vocal as well as his trumpet coda in the high register.

Mahogany Hall Stomp, taken at a fine medium tempo, has two themes. One is sixteen bars played by Louis at the beginning, and the other, regular twelve-bar blues played until the end with solos in the following order: one chorus by Louis, one by Charlie Holmes on alto saxophone, one by Lonnie Johnson on guitar, three by Louis with mute, one by Higginbotham on trombone, and two "open" trumpet choruses. Louis' playing, although very subtle, is a model of sobriety. His muted solo is unique for its kind. In the first of the three choruses Louis shows his amazing ability to create a real melody, perfectly developed on the harmonic chords of the blues. In the second chorus he holds a single note, just one, first diminuendo and then crescendo. He then repeats a typical New Orleans riff from beginning to end of the third chorus.

In July, 1929, Louis started a series of recordings in New York with Carroll Dickerson's band, which he brought from Chicago, eleven musicians strong. With such a number of musicians, ensemble arrangements replaced collective improvisations.

Despite such noticeable change, the seven interpretations recorded with Carroll Dickerson's orchestra retain the musical spirit of the previous recordings. They are

Ain't Misbehavin', Black and Blue, That Rhythm Man, Sweet Savannah Sue (four numbers composed by Fats Waller for the Connie's Inn *Hot Chocolates* show), *Some of These Days, When You're Smiling,* and *After You've Gone.* The reason is that, except for Earl Hines, all of the members of the Hot Five were now in Carroll Dickerson's band, as was Peter Briggs, the excellent tuba player of the Hot Seven. Louis is perfectly at home on both sides with the familiar New Orleans beat of Zutty and Peter Briggs. Zutty's drums come out best on *That Rhythm Man,* where his well-recorded breaks have a stimulating effect upon the other musicians.

All seven interpretations are outstanding. There are a few weak spots here and there, such as the short violin solos by Carroll Dickerson and a muted trumpet solo by Homer Hobson (the verse of *Sweet Savannah Sue*). But Louis is heard almost all the time, and what a Louis! He was probably in perfect physical condition, if one can judge by the power and mastery with which he performs solos full of difficulties. His first chorus on *Rhythm Man* and his last one on *Ain't Misbehavin'* have a tonal amplitude of singularly overwhelming effervescence.

Some of these recordings show Louis using more and more, and still better, the higher register of his instrument. In *When You're Smiling,* he plays the theme almost without variations, but in such a high register and with such fullness of sound that it created no less a sensation among the musicians than the most elaborate of Louis' choruses. It was even reproduced in a quicker tempo by Freddie Jenkins in Duke Ellington's *When You're Smiling.* In *Some of These Days,* too, Louis ends with a slight paraphrase of the theme executed in the high register with astonishing power. This chorus is even more striking because it immediately follows a trumpet chorus in which the low register of the horn is beautifully employed. The latter has been imitated by Dave Nelson in his recording of *Some of These Days*.

Although he makes more use of his mastery of high notes, there is still great variety in Louis' playing. How dedicated and relaxed he is in the first chorus of *After You've Gone!* The central break has been reproduced by many trumpet players. Bill Coleman quoted it in his own *After You've Gone* on His Master's Voice label. Louis' codas are, at the same time, so original and well turned that one could consider them part of the number, such as *The Rhythm Man* coda which has been copied a hundred times and reproduced on record often, as on Chick Webb's orchestral interpretation of *Rhythm Man*, for example.

In all these interpretations, Louis' voice is superbly recorded. The Okeh Company did the same excellent job in New York as in Chicago and Louis puts his heart and soul into every vocal. How can one stay cool while listening to the sublime vocal in *When You're Smiling* or remain inert to the swing of *After You've Gone*, with that same note repeated with different rhythmic nuances all the time? And what does one say of the vocal on *Black and Blue*, one of the most poignant, with its scat break recalling certain Jewish religious songs? That is where Louis sings of the misery of the blacks: "My only sin is in my skin, what did I do to be so black and blue?" and afterward, "I'm white inside, but that don't help my case. . . ."

Let me note that two different versions of *Some of These Days* and *When You're Smiling* were recorded on the same day and released simultaneously, one with vocal, one without. I have a weak spot for those on which Louis sings.

It is with Luis Russell's band in 1929–1930 that Louis recorded the following seven numbers: *I Ain't Got Nobody, Dallas Blues, St. Louis Blues, Rockin' Chair, Song of the Islands* and *Blue Turning Grey Over You.* They have an unusual sound because Paul Barbarin's snare drums were recorded very close to the microphone while Pope Foster continually uses the bow on his bass, both of them creating a typical New Orleans pulse. Except for a half-chorus by Higginbotham, *Blue Turning Grey Over You* is still Louis and one can tell that he has been inspired by this beautiful composition of Fats Waller.

The next seven numbers which were recorded in 1930 are *Dear Old Southland,* a trumpet solo accompanied by Buck Washington only on piano, *I Can't Believe That You're in Love With Me, My Sweet, Indian Cradle Song, Exactly Like You, Dinah,* and *Tiger Rag,* in which Louis is backed up by the Cocoanut Grove Orchestra.

Dear Old Southland is a masterpiece and an exception in Louis' recorded output because, except for the last chorus, it is not played in strict tempo. Louis improvises at will and Buck follows him step by step. Despite the absence of strict tempo, the interpretation belongs to the jazz idiom because of Louis' phrasing. He first plays the major-key theme of *Dear Old Southland* with some variation, notably in two sinuous and fast phrases showing his superb invention. Then he gets into the minor-key theme and plays it twice. He stays rather close to the theme, just filling in pauses in the melody with beautifully inventive phrases. Then Buck sets a regular tempo and Louis comes back to the major theme again, ending with a brilliant coda in the upper register.

Such an interpretation offers something unique: it is the only one where Louis' trumpet can be heard from beginning to end, and since there is only a piano with him, not one trumpet note is wasted. One can thoroughly enjoy Louis' tone, his vibrato being very much in the foreground during the numerous held notes. It is regrettable that Louis did not cut more records in the same circumstances.

The Cocoanut Grove Orchestra was one of the least satisfactory orchestras with which Louis recorded. The ensemble playing sometimes leaves something to be desired, especially in pitch accuracy. However, the band included some excellent musicians, such as Joe Turner on piano, Bernard Addison on guitar, and Cass McCord on tenor saxophone. But for the first time Louis is not backed by a rhythm section that gave him that New Orleans swing, which suited him best and which, thanks to Foster and Barbarin, he still maintained on those discs recorded with the Luis Russell Band.

Nevertheless, Louis Armstrong sings and plays so well in these recordings that one does not take much notice of the imperfections in the band. In *My Sweet*, Louis' playing stands out all the way through. Stating the theme on his trumpet with vibrating held notes, and singing with incredible verve which is also found in the impetuous trumpet chorus at the end, *My Sweet* might have been the greatest Louis Armstrong trumpet solo on disc, had it been better recorded (the band background tends to swamp the trumpet at times). In the other numbers made with the Cocoanut Grove band, Louis is featured about two-thirds of the time on each, except on *Tiger Rag*, where one has to wait a little too long for him. But then he plays two crazy trumpet choruses with most varied and unexpected quotations including a Scottish folk song *(The Campbells Are Coming)*, a popular foxtrot of the twenties *(Singing In the Rain)*, an American military march *(National Emblem)*, and an excerpt from comic opera *(I Pa-*

gliacci). These quotations fit so naturally with the development of the solo that one might not always be aware of them. In *Dinah,* Louis plays three trumpet choruses in a row—no less than ninety-six bars—which is rather exceptional even in his recording work and shows to advantage his endless invention and ability to build up a climax. The first of these choruses is extremely melodious. The second one leans more firmly on the beat, but there are still pretty phrases although most of them are more concise. In the third, with the band filling in, Louis uses still fewer notes and is at the height of his expressive power. This has to be included among Louis' greatest recorded trumpet solos. Another marvelous trumpet solo recorded with the Cocoanut Grove Orchestra is the last chorus of *I Can't Believe That You're in Love with Me,* which comes the closest to perfection of anything by Louis.

In the recordings made in 1930 in Los Angeles, Louis benefited from the support of a very gifted young drummer, Lionel Hampton.

The following interpretations have been recorded with Lawrence Brown on trombone: *I'm a Ding Dong Daddy, I'm in the Market for You, Confessin',* and *If I Could Be With You One Hour Tonight.* They are beautiful despite a whining Hawaiian guitar and a few hiccuping sounds made by a tenor saxophone.

I'm a Ding Dong Daddy is the most striking of the four recordings. What happened to Louis during his vocal chorus is a well-known story. Toward the middle of it he could not remember the words and started to sing "I done forgot the words," continuing the chorus with superb scat singing. This incident has been wrongly attributed to the 1926 recording of *Heebie Jeebies.** A little later Louis im-

*See page 70.

provises four trumpet choruses, giving astonishing power and inspiration to the last, just as in *Dinah* and other recordings in which he takes several choruses in a row, building up to a most impressive climax. This solo is one of Louis' most famous among musicians. Jonah Jones reproduced two of the choruses in his recording of *I'm a Ding Dong Daddy* with Sidney Bechet (on Blue Note). The beautiful *Confessin'* also has often been quoted by musicians as one of their favorite Armstrong records.

The following series, recorded with the Les Hite band in California (Lionel Hampton still on drums), included eight interpretations: *Body and Soul, Memories of You, You're Lucky to Me, Sweethearts on Parade, You're Driving Me Crazy, The Peanut Vendor, Just a Gigolo,* and *Shine.*

Good as each is, *Shine* tops them all. Louis plays the first chorus in fast tempo and sings the second in a slower one accompanied by Lionel Hampton, who plays vibraphone here instead of drums. A vocal break then leads back to the original tempo, followed by another chorus sung by Louis, who then plays the last two on trumpet. To introduce the last chorus Louis plays an incredible break-solo made up of a long glissando toward the higher register, one of those impressive exploits of Louis, "who could swing you into bad health," as Rex Stewart once said. The last chorus ends with a fantastic trumpet coda accompanied by just Lionel Hampton on drums. At first Louis leans toward the lower register, using several altered notes of unexpected effect; then he goes way up to end with biting high notes. This coda made such an impact on musicians that they used a similar device in numerous performances. One of the most famous examples is found at the end of Jimmie Lunceford's *Runnin' Wild*. The only defect in this masterpiece is that Louis' big trumpet volume is not recorded fully enough.

You're Driving Me Crazy begins with an amusing dialogue between Lionel Hampton and Louis. Lionel stutters so much that Louis acts as if he were affected by it, too, and assumes a very comical stutter (a quick example of Louis' ability as a comedian).

The Peanut Vendor is a rumba that Louis sings in the pure jazz idiom. He brings forth his whole self in the word *Marie*, bending the first syllable in a mischievous inflection toward the second syllable, held for a long time with Louis' inimitable vibrato.

On *Sweethearts on Parade*, Louis is featured all the way through. There are two trumpet choruses with a vocal chorus in between, all three magnificent. The way Louis has of stopping a note abruptly, which so many musicians were to imitate, is much in evidence at the beginning of his vocal and in his last chorus.

Louis' voice comes through in all its beauty in the vocal of *Body and Soul*. It is particularly intriguing to hear the manly voice of Louis Armstrong singing with nostalgia in *I'm Just a Gigolo*.

Now we come to the last series of Louis Armstrong's recordings for the Okeh Company: twenty-four sides made in 1931–1932 with a nine-piece band which, although formed in Chicago, was made up mostly of New Orleans musicians.

No one will probably ever know why this band played much better in the first eight interpretations than in the others, for not one musician was subsequently changed. Anyhow, Louis is again backed up by a rhythm section swinging in the New Orleans style. Unfortunately, Tubby Hall's great drumming is under-recorded, while the not too supple guitar tempo of Mike McKendrick is reproduced too loudly. Preston Jackson, the trombone player,

had trouble with his lips at the time, and the three saxophonists, good individually, were not successful as a section. Zilmer Randolph, the second trumpet player and
also the straw boss of the band, wrote good arrangements,
although some of them do not sound too good, probably
due to unsatisfactory ensemble playing.

The first eight interpretations in which the band played
acceptably are: *Walking My Baby Back Home, I Surrender, Dear, When It's Sleepy Time Down South, Blue
Again, Little Joe, You Rascal You, Them There Eyes*, and
When Your Lover Has Gone. Evolution is detectable in
Louis' playing. After the increasingly audacious and impetuous improvisations on *I'm a Ding Dong Daddy* and
Shine, it seems Louis was now close to the point where he
reached his musical maturity. Instead of indulging in further exploration, the time seemed to have come for him
to install himself in the conquered land and adjust to his
own needs and means. His style is the same, but the inner
accent is now serene and dominating. The wild exuber-
ance of youth vanishes, giving place to the superior mastery of the skilled man. Never had Louis' supremacy been
shown so clearly as in *Blue Again, When Your Lover Has
Gone*, and *When It's Sleepy Time Down South*. He plays
and sings all through the numbers, and it is hard to decide
which one should admire the most, his trumpet or his
vocals, for both are so moving and creative. The way he
swings is more imperious than ever. His genius for setting
a tempo is simply fantastic, for example, in the beginning
of the last chorus of *Blue Again*, and on *When Your Lover
Has Gone*. Louis quotes a part of his famous *West End
Blues* opening in the magnificent introduction to *Blue
Again*. He ends with descending phrases, including half-
tones, which were to become the daily bread of trumpet
players, saxophonists, and other instrumentalists. Among

others, *I Surrender, Dear* and *Little Joe* are in the same vein as the previous numbers. Louis paraphrases the theme of *Walkin' My Baby Back Home* with delicate sensitivity and his last two choruses on *Them There Eyes* (vocal and trumpet) have made a tremendous impression upon musicians.

As for *You Rascal You,* it is a masterpiece of a new kind. Louis improvises the most staggering vocal variations, extending them to the lyrics themselves. He even adds his own words of cynical humor, "I'll be standing on the corner high when they bring your body by." Few records equal this masterpiece in its full revelation of Louis' vocal capabilities.

The sixteen interpretations that follow are sometimes uneven. The saxophone section is often at fault, as if the musicians tried to catch on with one another without always succeeding in being together. These mistakes spoil parts of *Georgia On My Mind* and *You Can Depend On Me,* as well as short parts of *Kicking the Gong Around, Love You Funny Thing,* and *Keepin' Out of Mischief Now,* but Louis plays and sings as beautifully as ever.

Chinatown is one of the very few discs on which Louis makes extended use of brilliant technical virtuosity. The attack and swing with which Louis repeats a few notes in the high register are of galvanizing intensity. The four trumpet choruses of this record were harmonized and played by Earl Hines' trumpet section, but Earl's band never had a chance to record it.

New Tiger Rag is an interpretation of the same type as *Chinatown* but the tempo is much faster; in fact it is incredibly fast. Louis takes seven and a half choruses, obtaining a beautiful effect by playing most of the time as if the tempo were half as fast. Some choruses are built on only two or three notes held with gorgeous vibrato or shaped with terrific swing.

Louis sings and plays wonderfully on *Home,* but the sound of the band behind him is not too happy. *Lonesome Road* has Louis in the role of a minister preaching in a humorous way and cracking comical jokes while his musicians answer vocally and instrumentally for the congregation. In *I Got Rhythm,* almost every musician in the band takes a short solo as Louis names each in turn. Then he takes up his trumpet for the last two choruses.

The best interpretations of this series are *Lazy River,* in which Louis sings two choruses (the second, scatted, is a small wonder in itself); *Wrap Your Troubles in Dreams,* animated by the same grandiose inspiration as *Blue Again* and *When Your Lover Has Gone; All of Me* and *Between the Devil and the Deep Blue Sea,* in both of which Louis plays highly inspired muted solos with melodious, fast, fluent phrases that show he can play as fast as anybody when he wants to; *Stardust;** and finally *Lawd, You Made the Night Too Long,* the last recording of the series, which is also the greatest. It is a masterpiece—one of the most dramatic among Louis' work. From the start the three "hallelujahs" stun the listener with their emotion. Then comes a deep, intense solo in the low register of the trumpet; and then, the vocal. The way Louis sings here is a climax in jazz music. He gets back to the theme on his vehement trumpet and then tops the interpretation majestically with a coda perfectly appropriate to the general trend of the number.

More so than *Blue Again* and the masterpieces re-

---

*Two versions, recorded the same day, have been released of *Stardust,* as well as of *Wrap Your Troubles in Dreams* and *Between the Devil and the Deep Blue Sea.* The comparisons these afford show the extent to which Louis Armstrong creates from take to take of each number.

corded a few months earlier, *Lawd, You Made the Night Too Long* strikingly reveals that fugitive moment when the flowering of youth and the life-awareness of the mature man were coexistent in Louis' music. Youth was in evidence in the preceding recordings, while maturity was to take over in those that followed; but right there, in *Lawd, You Made the Night Too Long,* the two aspects of Louis' personality faced one another and mysteriously combined.

Lawd, You Made the Night Too Long is, alas, for quite a while the last number in which Louis' voice is recorded as it should be. He stopped recording for the Okeh Company (which was soon to disappear), and his next records were released under the Victor label, and after that on that of Decca. Strange as it may seem, for several years the engineers of these record companies were not able to record Louis' voice as well as their colleagues at the Okeh Company.

Louis' first recordings for Victor in 1932 were a *Medley of Armstrong Hits,* made with a Philadelphia orchestra, and four numbers with Chick Webb's band: *That's My Home, Hobo, You Can't Ride This Train, I Hate to Leave You Now,* and *You'll Wish You'd Never Been Born.*

Medley of Armstrong Hits was released on two sides of a twelve-inch 78 record. The mediocre recording (and the band is not too good either) makes for disappointing listening. Louis plays and sings beautiful choruses, however, especially in *When It's Sleepy Time Down South.* This part of the medley was long enough to allow the Victor Company to release it later, separately, on a ten-inch 78 single.

Of the four interpretations with Chick Webb, the best is *That's My Home* in which Louis improvises beautiful trumpet variations, strongly supported by Chick Webb's drums and Elmer James' tuba. *I Hate to Leave You Now*, a pleasant melody composed by Fats Waller and Louis Armstrong, is also sung and played in a moving way. *Hobo* is well sung by Louis and well swung by the band, but the other number is not as successful.

Later on, Victor released different versions of *That's My Home*, and *I Hate to Leave You Now*, recorded on the same day, which offer another example of Louis' inventiveness in improvisation. The trumpet solos, especially of *That's My Home*, are almost entirely different.

The other Victor interpretations—twenty-three in all—were recorded during the first months of 1933 with a band organized for Louis in Chicago by Zilmer Randolph. It included several excellent musicians, among them Teddy Wilson on piano (only on the first twelve sides), Scoville Browne on alto saxophone, and the Johnson Brothers (Keg and Budd) on trombone and tenor saxophone respectively. The trouble with this band was that it did not execute the arranged ensembles very well; also, the recording is confused. Fortunately, the trumpet stands out well on most of the numbers. Louis' playing is more powerful than ever during this period. It seems that he has never blown with such strength or produced such enormous volume from his horn. There are notable solos in *I Gotta Right to Sing the Blues* and *Dusky Stevedore*, and amazing codas in *Mississippi Basin, He's a Son of the South*, and *Sittin' in the Dark*.

If the new version of *St. Louis Blues* cannot be compared with the original Okeh version, that of *Basin Street Blues* is almost as great as the 1928 version, except for the recording. As for *Mahogany Hall Stomp*, Louis' inspiration is as superb here as in the Okeh version, which is saying much. When one knows the latter by heart one cannot help but marvel at all the new things Louis has to say on the same number despite the fact that the routine of the performance is the same. For instance, in the third muted chorus, instead of the riff used in the original version, a repeated glissando is made and swung in a remarkably subtle way.

Next to *Mahogany Hall Stomp,* the best of these Victor recordings are *Snowball,* spoken, sung and played by Louis in a very moving way, and *Some Sweet Day,* which contains the best trombone chorus Keg Johnson ever recorded. A special mention should be made of *Laughin' Louis,* a sort of comic sketch at the end of which Louis plays an unaccompanied trumpet solo with a beautiful melodic line—a solo about which musicians are still raving.

The next six interpretations were recorded in Paris in 1934 by the Brunswick Company. The band, a new one organized in Europe, is no improvement on the last, but the recording is at least quite clear. The best interpretation is that which features Louis the most, *On the Sunny Side of the Street.* Louis had not recorded this number before but had been performing it for several years, which explains why Taft Jordon had been able to imitate Louis' vocal and trumpet solo in *On the Sunny Side of the Street* when he recorded it (with Chick Webb's band) before Louis himself had done so. The other numbers made in Paris are *Super Tiger Rag, St. Louis Blues, Will You Won't You Be My Baby,* and *Song of the Vipers.* The last title is a very original composition by Louis Armstrong offering a marvelous trumpet part that made the best possible use of the high register. The last solo of *Song of the Vipers* gives a pretty good idea of the Louis Armstrong Parisians heard at his first two concerts in France.

After a year without making any discs, Louis began to record again for Decca, with whom he was to stay for about ten years.

The beginning was not a very happy one. Luis Russell's band which had again become Louis' orchestra was not at its best despite the presence of excellent jazzmen like Pops Foster and Paul Barbarin, who were often under-recorded. Most of the time Louis' discs for Decca lack volume and his voice comes out very muffled. In addition, the Decca people asked Louis to record some rather poor quality hits of the day: *Rhythm Saved the World, La Cucaracha, Music Goes Round and Round*, etc. But Louis' trumpet playing, renewed again, is more beautiful than ever. Generally leaving aside high-note effects, he concentrated on conciseness with still greater mastery, reaching a composure and tone accuracy never before obtained with such perfectioñ. A new era started where Louis Armstrong the Fighter now became Louis Armstrong the Champion. Before, his career was a matter of seeking and finding. Now, he *knows*. He is above the struggle. In short, he can now express the meaning of what he did before with a more intricate, moving melodic line. Such conciseness allows a maximum of swing in execution.

Of the first of Louis' Decca records, *You're My Lucky Star* and *Old Man Mose* are tops. The first one has a penetrating and insinuating swing to the vocal, followed by a trumpet chorus in a faster tempo. It is amazing to hear the authority with which Louis sets the new tempo by just one note played several times on the beat with strong attack. All the rest of the chorus is full of invention, each idea being perfectly developed.

Two versions of *Old Man Mose* recorded on the same day have been issued. One opens with a rather awkward arrangement; then Louis sings the verse and the chorus twice with vocal replies from his musicians. The other version begins with an overwhelming trumpet solo, followed by the same singing routine but in a faster tempo. The latter version would certainly be the best if Louis' voice was not muffled even more here than in the other.

Red Sails in the Sunset and *On Treasure Island* are enchanting for Louis (Paul Barbarin's drums, for once well recorded in *On Treasure Island*). But the first wholly successful Decca session is the one which produced *Thanks a Million*, which opens with a singing, lyrical trumpet solo including a breathtaking incursion into the upper register. *I Hope Gabriel Likes My Music* ends with a bubbling trumpet chorus that electrified the entire band. In *Solitude* and *Shoe Shine Boy* Louis' voice was better recorded than previously, so that now we are favored with a beautiful vocal in both numbers.

If We Never Meet Again is a charming number composed by Louis Armstrong. A tenor saxophone states the theme while Louis fills in with beautiful improvisations on trumpet (muted); then Louis takes a stunning vocal.

On the session of May 18, 1936, the quality of the recording improved again. The Decca engineers took care to have Foster's bass heard, and the band did not sound as if it were playing in another room. If the new version of *Mahogany Hall Stomp* is not as outstanding as the two previous ones, *Lying to Myself, Ev'ntide, Thankful, Red Nose*, and *Swing That Music* show Louis in top form all the way through. The recording of Louis' voice, though not as good as on the Okeh records, has regained warmth and vitality. *Swing That Music*, taken at a really fast tempo, contains no less than four trumpet choruses, and in the last ones Louis blows up a storm.*

*Louis also recorded *Swing That Music* with Jimmie Dorsey's orchestra several months later, but the version with his own band is better.

During the same year the Decca Company also recorded Louis with orchestras other than his own. That is why in February, 1936, Louis cut two numbers, *I'm Putting All My Eggs in One Basket* and *Yes, Yes, My, My,* with white musicians. The rhythm section is weak. Nevertheless, *I'm Putting All My Eggs in One Basket* is among the best interpretations of the year. Louis' unaccompanied trumpet introduction is highly original and the way he states the theme is the very substance of swing.

Of the five numbers recorded in California in August, 1936, with Jimmy Dorsey's orchestra, *The Skeleton in the Closet* (from the film *Pennies from Heaven*) is the most successful. Jimmy Dorsey's band, if more precise than Luis Russell's, does not swing as much, most notably on *Dipper Mouth Blues,* where Louis does not play at great length. However, this interpretation is interesting because Louis plays the three famous King Oliver choruses which he had already used in the 1925 recording of *Sugar Foot Stomp* (another title for *Dipper Mouth Blues*) with Fletcher Henderson. A comparison of the two solos reveals Louis' evolution. As the musical text is the same except for a few notes here and there, the main difference, and it's a big one, is the way these phrases are executed. In the Fletcher Henderson version, although he already had perfect control, Louis played the three choruses with the impetuous flame of youth. In the other he played more imposingly and serenely. Each note bears the weight of his entire life, with its joys and sorrows. The Louis phrases you already know strike deeper because their fullness and expressive power have been enhanced by his experience of life.

The Decca people had the strange idea of recording Louis in California during 1936 with Hawaiian-style groups performing the exotic numbers, *To You Sweetheart Aloha* and *On a Cocoanut Island*. They followed these with *On a Little Bamboo Bridge* and *Hawaiian Hospitality* in New York in 1937. Despite the Hawaiian guitar and a few other strange sounds in the background, Louis continued imperturbably on his own way as if he were surrounded by real jazz musicians.

The year 1937 saw the recording of four numbers with the famous vocal quartet, the Mills Brothers. One performance of *Darling Nelly Gray* is to be ranked among Louis' best of the period. It ends with a long coda in which Louis sings exactly as he plays his horn. Two different versions have been issued of it. The three other interpretations, *Carry Me Back to Old Virginny*, *In the Shade of the Old Apple Tree*, and *The Old Folks at Home* are also superb examples of Louis' singing and trumpet playing, but so far as swing is concerned, the Mills Brothers are left far behind.

In July, 1937, after more than a year away from the studio, Louis again began to record with his own band. Thanks to the improvement of the band and of Decca's recording techniques, the discs sound better. *Yours and Mine* and *Sun Showers* are excellent and each contains a triumphant trumpet chorus. Louis sings and plays like nobody's business in *Public Melody No. I*, from the film *Artists and Models*. And when it came to interpreting rumbas like *Cuban Pete* and *She's the Daughter of a Planter from Havana*, he transposed them into the jazz idiom, swinging them as much as any other number. The two trumpet choruses on *Havana* are even among the most inspired of this period.

But it is toward the end of 1937 and the beginning of 1938 that Louis made in California what could be considered his most beautiful recordings since the famous ones of 1925–1932. *On the Sunny Side of the Street* is the first. After a fine Higginbotham trombone solo Louis took a vocal chorus and played one and a half choruses on trumpet, every note of which spelled perfection—another of his great solos.

Next came a batch of wonderful recordings: *Jubilee*, from the film *Every Day's a Holiday* with Mae West, on which Louis rides with incredible ease in the high register for his two trumpet choruses; *Struttin' with Some Barbecue*, the good tune recorded ten years earlier by the Hot Five, which ends with two bursting trumpet choruses. This interpretation is marred only by an out-of-tune clarinet solo. Other good ones are *The Trumpet Player's Lament, Let That Be a Lesson to You, I Double Dare You*, and *Sweet As a Song*, the latter showing how Louis can turn a rather poor sentimental song into deeply moving music. *Satchelmouth Swing*, the old *Coal Cart Blues* of the Clarence Williams Blue Five, is less interesting because Louis is not featured enough, but the band sounds good here.

The next series includes eight numbers from *So Little Time* to *Love Walked In* and gave us the first and best recorded interpretation of the now famous *When the Saints Go Marching In*. Higginbotham plays two majestic trombone solos; Paul Barbarin, who is at his best, swings at the drums in typical New Orleans fashion; and the entire band is almost worthy of its leader.

During that same year, 1938, Decca recorded Louis Armstrong again with the most varied groups. First there were three new numbers with the Mills Brothers: *Flat Foot Floogie, The Song Is Ended*, and *My Walking Stick*. Although a little less successful than the previous recordings with the Mills Brothers, they were often illuminated by Louis' vitality.

Then come four spirituals with the Lyn Murray choir, *Shadrack, Going to Shout All Over God's Heaven, Jonah and the Whale,* and *Nobody Knows the Trouble I've Seen.* The way the choir sings has very little to do with the style of authentic gospel singers, but it is a kick to hear Louis singing these numbers which differ so much from all his other performances up until then. In *Nobody Knows the Trouble I've Seen* his singing is a real prayer, while he delivers the picturesque lyrics of *Shadrack* and *Jonah* with incomparable humor.

Elder Eatmore's Sermons are sermons humorously spoken by Louis. His voice could have been recorded better, but it is good to have these two sermons, for Louis talks as meaningfully as he sings.

Then there were four numbers recorded with a white studio group, *Naturally, I've Got a Pocket Full of Dreams, Ain't Misbehavin',* and *I Can't Give You Anything But Love,* the last completely different from the earlier Okeh version.

Finally, there are two numbers with the Casa Loma orchestra: *Lazy Bones,* on which Louis is heard very little, and *Rockin' Chair,* on which his trumpet is not too well recorded, but the vocal sounds fine. The Casa Loma Orchestra is rather lymphatic.

At the beginning of 1939, Louis began recording with his own band again. Paul Barbarin was replaced by Sidney Catlett, one of the greatest drummers in the history of jazz, and his playing adds a lot to the interpretations.

After the first two numbers, *Jeepers Creepers* and *What Is This Thing Called Swing,* both equally successful, Louis was asked to record six of the numbers that he had made for Okeh during the 1920s: *Heah Me Talkin' to Ya, Save It Pretty Mama, West End Blues, Savoy Blues, Confessin',* and *Monday Date.* The old Okeh records had become very rare and were much in demand; many jazz fans were trying to obtain copies of them. That is probably what gave the Decca people the idea of having Louis again cut these numbers. But these new versions were not what fans were asking for; they wanted the original versions.

That does not mean that the Decca remakes were not good—far from it—but in jazz it is not the number performed which makes the music, it is the way it is played. Made ten to twelve years later with different musicians, these numbers sounded entirely changed, even those in which the band tried to come close to the original versions, which was the case with *West End Blues* and *Savoy Blues.* Except for one chorus in each, the last one in *Savoy Blues* and the one before the last in *West End Blues,* Louis closely followed the old versions. Yet he plays them in a very different way, especially the two middle choruses of *Savoy Blues.* Although most phrases are the same in the Okeh version, the accent is altogether different, just as Louis' solo in *Dipper Mouth* with Jimmy Dorsey differed from the one in Fletcher Henderson's *Sugar Foot Stomp.*

In the other numbers Louis Armstrong did not follow the old recordings approximately but created new music. His three choruses on *Save It Pretty Mama,* one sung, two on trumpet, are just as beautiful as the old ones. *Heah Me Talkin' to Ya* is taken at a faster tempo than the original version and the solos, except Louis', are not so outstanding. But *Confessin'* almost equals the Okeh recording and *Monday Date* is superb for Louis.

Two other numbers were recorded at the same time, *If It's Good,* which contains a *swinging* trumpet chorus, and *Me and Brother Bill,* entirely sung, which gets a comical kind of treatment.

30. Louis as guest on NBC's Tonight Show, late 1960s.

31. ABOVE. Backstage at New York's Latin Quarter. Pearl Bailey, Pearl's husband, drummer Louis Bellson, and Louis, 1967.

32. BELOW. "Salute to Satchmo Nite" at Newport Jazz Festival, July, 1970. Mahalia Jackson and Louis.

33. "Salute to Satchmo Nite" at Newport Jazz Festival, July, 1970. Louis, Jack Lesberg, Bobby Hackett.

34.   Louis rehearsing at Newport Jazz Festival, 1970.

35. Rehearsal at Newport Jazz Festival, July 1970. Bobby Hackett, Captain John Handy, Dizzy Gillespie, George Wein.

36. Louis in Chicago, circa 1929.

38. Louis, early 1960s.

After the next session in June of 1939, which produced two excellent interpretations, *Baby Won't You Please Come Home* and *Shanty Boat on the Mississippi*, we come to two of the best sessions Louis ever made for Decca. The recording is very good and the band really swings, with Louis in top form; everything goes superbly.

The first of these two sessions, December, 1939, included *You're a Lucky Guy, You're Just a No Account, Poor Old Joe*, and *Bye and Bye*. The trumpet chorus in *You're Just a No Account* recalls the days of *When Your Lover Has Gone* and *Blue Again*, in terms of both melodic and rhythmic character. The entire band, irresistibly pushed ahead by the first-class rhythm section, magnificently led by Sidney Catlett and Pops Foster, really swings like the best big bands of the period, supporting Louis better than it ever had before, especially in *You're a Lucky Guy* and *Bye and Bye*. This latter recording ends with three crazy trumpet choruses. Louis builds up to the climax reached in the last chorus when he powerfully swings the same three high notes from beginning to end of the chorus.

Then came the session of March, 1940, during which *Hep Cat's Ball, Harlem Stomp, Lazy 'Sippi River, Wolverine Blues*, and *You've Got Me Voodoed* were recorded, all of them as exciting and successful as the previous interpretations. The second half of *Wolverine Blues* is made up of a long trumpet solo, two and a half choruses —eighty bars, developed with perfect logic. This is the solo that opened the eyes, or rather the ears, of those who thought (I still wonder why) that Louis' creative gift had decreased since the Okeh period.

Another session with the Mills Brothers resulted in *Boog It, Cherry, Marie*, and *W.P.A.* Along with *Darling Nelly Gray, Cherry* stands out as the best number recorded by Louis Armstrong with the Mills Brothers. His singing is deeply moving and his trumpet chorus is full of serenity.

The next session by Louis with his regular band gave us *You'll Ruin Your Mouth* and *Cut Off My Legs,* both entertaining numbers where Louis, in high spirits, displayed his verve in a half-spoken, half-sung style. *Sweethearts On Parade* is not as good as the old version, and last but not least, *Cain and Abel* is a masterpiece where Louis can be heard in a grandiose trumpet solo featuring a few very moving altered notes, backed up in an impressive way by Sidney Catlett's drumming.

In May, 1940, Decca decided to organize a New Orleans session with Louis (it was the beginning of what was called the New Orleans Revival). So they surrounded him with a pick-up group composed of Sidney Bechet (soprano saxophone and clarinet), Claude Jones (trombone), Luis Russell (piano), Bernard Addison (guitar), Wellman Braud (bass), and Zutty Singleton (drums). It is enchanting to hear Louis again with first-class New Orleans musicians such as Zutty, Bechet, and Braud. The numbers recorded were *2:19 Blues, Down in Honky Tonk Town, Perdido Street Blues,* and *Coal Cart Blues.*

2:19 Blues, a twelve-bar blues in slow tempo, is the real low-down blues. In the first and last chorus Bechet and Claude Jones complement Louis' nonchalant statement of the tune very well. Bechet plays one chorus on soprano saxophone and Louis sings two, creating remarkable tension and swinging in an unforgettable way.

Down in Honky Tonk Town includes two beautiful solos, one by Bechet, one by Zutty, while a chorus is split between Claude Jones and Addison. But the most memorable point of this interpretation is the three ensemble choruses; two at the beginning, which Louis leads, stating the theme with strong attack and pulsation, and one at the end where Louis improvises beautiful variations. Bechet plays a pleasing counterpoint to the trumpet part with very bright ideas, but at times he gives the impression of wanting to outshine Louis. In fact, that was the impression of one of the musicians on that date, who later said: "Can you imagine such a thing, Bechet trying to cut Louis?"

Perdido Street Blues is a little less successful because the piano and guitar solos sound rather weak coming after the powerful playing by Louis and Bechet (on clarinet here) at the beginning of the interpretation. But then toward the end Louis cuts loose with three driving trumpet choruses.

The reason why *Coal Cart Blues* does not compare with the other three interpretations is that it was played by only Louis, Bechet, Braud and Addison. It was a bad idea to eliminate Zutty; without his swinging drumming this performance has not the punch or verve of the others.

The next eight numbers recorded in 1941 were also played by a small group, but this time the six musicians involved were taken from Louis' band: George Washington (trombone), Prince Robinson (clarinet), Luis Russell (piano), John Williams (bass), Lawrence Lucie (guitar), and Sidney Catlett (drums). Two of these interpretations are especially good, *Hey Lawdy Mama*, an old-time blues which Louis sings as it was never sung before, and *Now Do You Call That a Buddy*, a masterpiece. In the first sixteen bars Louis' tone, in a rather low register, is more beautiful than ever and he makes his instrument "talk" in a deeply moving way. He then sings three verses and three choruses in a dramatic style which has a poignant effect upon the listener. This would be one of the best vocals by Louis on disc if his voice had been recorded slightly better.

The six other interpretations contain excellent passages, especially a scintillating trumpet chorus in *Long, Long Ago*, masterfully supported by John Williams and Sidney Catlett.

Louis is again heard with his entire band in two subsequent sessions. The first one gave us a new version of *You Rascal You* and *When It's Sleepy Time Down South*, the latter without vocal, and it is the only version of this often recorded number by Louis (it was to become his signature tune) in which he does not sing. Then there is *I Used to Love You*, taken in an unexpected slow tempo where Louis plays the theme without altering it much, but with a kind of low-down accent usually used for the blues. Finally there is *Leap Frog*, which is of little interest since Louis takes only eight bars in it. It has been said that there is another pressing of this number which has a lot of trumpet on it, but I have never been able to lay my hands on it.

The four numbers from the other session in April, 1942, *Coquette, Among My Souvenirs, I Never Knew*, and *Cash for Your Trash*, were to be the last Armstrong recordings for over two years, because all recording in the United States was halted during this period due to a disagreement between the Musician's Union and the big record companies.

Louis stepped into the Decca recording studio again on August 9, 1944. Of the three numbers cut on that day, only one has been released (and not until twenty-five years after the actual recording), *Groovin'*, a swinging interpretation without vocal featuring Louis' trumpet well. However, the first Armstrong records to be released since those in 1942 were *I Wonder* and *Jodie Man*, recorded in January, 1945, with a white studio band that fortunately was much better than those used during the '30s. Louis' voice is a little muffled by the recording but he works miracles with Cecil Gant's pretty number, *I Wonder.*

The last records of this first Decca period were *You Won't Be Satisfied* and *The Frim Fram Sauce.* This time the Decca people had the grand notion of teaming Louis Armstrong with that wonderful singer, Ella Fitzgerald, and it is a real pleasure to hear them together.

1946 saw the return of Louis as an exclusive RCA-Victor artist. First he appeared on two sides of a twelve-inch 78 with an all-star band made up mostly of musicians selected as the best of the year by *Esquire* magazine, among them Duke Ellington, Johnny Hodges, Don Byas, and Billy Strayhorn. Unfortunately the session was under the supervision of Leonard Feather, who took this opportunity to have Louis sing blues with lyrics which he, Leonard, had composed—those on *Long Long Journey,* which are a poor imitation of genuine and often very poetic black blues lyrics. Louis has a hard time trying to make such lyrics meaningful. On the other number, *Snafu,* Louis plays a beautiful trumpet chorus.

During 1946 and 1947 Louis carried out three sessions for RCA-Victor with his regular band. The first gave us the original version of *Back o' Town Blues,* which was so successful that ever since it has been a standard piece at all his concerts. Louis' band, including many newcomers, most of them young, swung well, but the recording did not do it justice. However, Louis' voice is well recorded. Next to *Back o' Town Blues,* the best disc of this session is *Joseph 'n' His Brudders.*

During those same two years Victor also recorded Louis with small pick-up groups in *Sugar* and *I Want a Little*

Girl as well as on two blues. Vic Dickenson, Barney Bigard, Zutty Singleton and three other musicians are Louis' partners. Some numbers recorded live at a concert at Town Hall in New York on May 17, 1947, featured Louis with white musicians, except for Sidney Catlett on drums, who was sometimes replaced by George Wettling. Another pick-up group, including among others Jack Teagarden, Cozy Cole, Al Casey, and Al Hall, recorded four interpretations in June, 1947. Among them were *Jack-Armstrong Blues*, which ends with several overwhelming trumpet choruses in the high register, and *Some Day*, a pretty tune composed by Louis Armstrong, who has himself told how the melody came to him while he was dreaming. As soon as he awoke he noted down the lyrics and music to be sure that he did not forget them. This number, which received little attention at first, was later to be included in the repertoire of many jazzmen.

But the best of all these sessions with small pick-up groups was that which took place in October, 1946. Louis recorded three of the tunes which he was performing in the movie *New Orleans* with the very same musicians who surrounded him in the film except for Zutty, who was unavailable, and he was replaced by another great New Orleans drummer, Minor Hall. With the latter, Kid Ory (trombone), Barney Bigard (clarinet), and Budd Scott (guitar), Louis was back with a really first-class New Orleans band. *Do You Know What It Means to Miss New Orleans?*, a new version of *Mahogany Hall Stomp*, and *Where the Blues Were Born in New Orleans* were cut at that session, and the last interpretation is certainly to be remembered among the best of this period. The three last choruses of collective improvisation are particularly breathtaking and show that these New Orleans musicians were full of new ideas, for their music, although just as authentic, was

entirely different from anything they played during the
'20s.

Louis' big orchestra was disbanded during the summer
of 1947 and it was with his new regular group, the Louis
Armstrong All Stars, that he recorded his last sides for
Victor in October, 1947: *A Song Is Born, Lovely Weather
We're Havin', Please Stop Playing the Blues,* and *Before
Long,* the first two being the best.

In the meantime Louis had recorded some perfor-
mances for the American Armed Forces on the famous V
Discs (Victory Discs) which were not for general release,
but to entertain the soldiers overseas—in Europe and
Asia. Two numbers, *Confessin'* and *Jack-Armstrong
Blues,* were made specially; others were parts of concerts
given in New York, *Black and Blue* and *Rockin' Chair*
(Carnegie Hall concert of February 8, 1947). *Basin Street
Blues, Back o' Town Blues,* and *Flyin' on a V-Disc* were
extracts from the celebrated January 26, 1944, concert at
the Metropolitan Opera House in New York by an all-star
band selected by *Esquire.* The musicians included Art
Tatum, Coleman Hawkins, Oscar Pettiford, Al Casey, Sidney Catlett, Roy Eldridge, Lionel Hampton, and others.
Years later some jazz fans succeeded in getting the recording of the entire *Esquire* concert and circulated un-
derground copies.* In the same way, many of Louis'
broadcasts, recorded by enthusiastic fans (also by some
people who were not fans of the music but more interested in money) appeared on pirate records, but we shall
not deal with these here for most of them are too badly
recorded. Some of them, of course, give one a chance to

---

*The fact that a dozen illustrious jazzmen were playing at this con-
cert confused many people as to the value of the music. There were,
of course, some great moments but many weak parts, too.

hear amazing solos by Louis, such as three tremendous trumpet choruses on *Heebie Jeebies,* played during a broadcast on August 3, 1949.

During 1948 a new disagreement between the Musicians' Union and the recording companies kept Louis away from the recording studios.

There was, however, one exception. When Louis participated during the week in the very first International Jazz Festival on the French Riviera in February, 1948, organized by the town of Nice and the French Radio Network, some of his concerts were recorded for radio broadcasts. The following year *L'Association Française de Gramophilie* obtained permission to release a few extracts from these concerts on record, and these records testify to the high quality of jazz played in Nice by Louis and his musicians. *Panama, Royal Garden Blues, A Monday Date, Black and Blue, Velma's Blues,* and *That's My Desire* are beautiful discs despite recording mistakes such as too much bass and not enough drums. *That's My Desire,* a vocal duet between Louis Armstrong and Velma Middleton, is one of the best ever.

In 1949, Louis again became an exclusive Decca artist. The Decca people thinking, rightly or wrongly, that the jazz being played by the regular Louis Armstrong All Stars was not going to sell well, preferred to record him with various studio bands. Sometimes these were composed of excellent jazz musicians as was the case for *Maybe It's Because* and *I'll Keep the Love Light Burning.* Sometimes there was a choir singing in a style which had little to do with jazz, but this was when we got *Blueberry Hill* and *That Lucky Old Sun,* on which Louis did not play trumpet at all but sang magnificently (vocal records were selling better at the time). Decca was well rewarded for *Blueberry Hill,* a best seller.

In 1950, the recordings of *C'est Si Bon* and *La Vie en Rose* with a big studio band were also very successful commercially. Here Louis Armstrong is in top form, playing trumpet as much as he sings. His subtle paraphrase of the theme of *La Vie en Rose*, a popular French song not in the jazz idiom, is a perfect demonstration of that often forgotten maxim: in jazz music it is not the tune that counts most, but the way in which it is played. These two interpretations are successful, the more so since the recording does full justice to Louis' voice and horn. From then on most of Louis' Decca discs were well recorded and his voice was no longer muffled.

Decca also recorded Louis with various singers: with Louis Jordon and his band in a new version of *You Rascal You* in which the grandiose trumpet introduction amazed the musicians; with Bing Crosby *(Gone Fishing)*, with Billie Holiday *(My Sweet Hunk o' Trash)*, and with Ella Fitzgerald. The first session with Ella in 1950 gave us the charming *Can Anyone Explain?* and *Dream a Little Dream on Me*. The second session, in 1951, produced *Oops* and three other numbers but was less successful.

Although it took the Decca people a long time to record Louis with his own singer, Velma Middleton, they did at last manage it in 1951, with *You're Just in Love, Big Butter and Egg Man,* and *You're the Apple of My Eye.* Although Velma was not an Ella Fitzgerald, she had a great affinity with Louis and was, for him, a more appropriate partner. *You're Just in Love* is a little gem.

From 1950 onward 33-rpm microgroove records allowed Louis to be heard in long-playing interpretations, not with pick-up groups but heading his regular combo composed of Jack Teagarden (trombone), Barney Bigard (clarinet), Earl Hines (piano), Arvell Shaw (bass), and Cozy Cole (drums).

Two ten-inch LPs came out of those sessions in April, 1950. One of them included two short interpretations, *My Bucket's Got a Hole in It* and *Panama*, and two long ones, *New Orleans Function*, a beautiful and picturesque reconstruction of the music which used to be played at funerals in New Orleans (going and returning from the cemetery), and *Bugle Call Rag*, which, besides an abundant drums solo by Cozy Cole—amazing for its swing as well as for his instrumental virtuosity—features at length Louis' trumpet playing at its best. This was the first record released which gives one an exact idea of the music played by Louis and his band at their concerts and dances.

The other LP was also a reflection of Louis' concerts— another aspect of them: the specialty numbers starring individually the musicians of the band. Earl Hines shines on piano in *Fine and Dandy*, Jack Teagarden plays and sings on *Baby, Won't You Please Come Home*, Barney Bigard plays a lot of clarinet on *I Surrender Dear*, while Arvell Shaw and Cozy Cole are featured on *Russian Lullaby*. As for Louis, he plays and sings all the way through *That's for Me*, one of his most moving recordings of this period.*

The next Louis Armstrong LPs released by Decca were recordings of concerts by the All Stars; *Satchmo at Symphony Hall*,† on a double LP, seemingly gave the entire

---

*It should be noted that the recordings of April, 1950, packed in two homogenous LPs, were later reissued in various twelve-inch LPs with other recordings made at other sessions. Since LPs were invented jazz fans have been the victims of most illogical repackagings; a lot of LPs are made up of two or three numbers included in a previous LP mixed with others first issued in other LPs, so that it is almost impossible for fans to get all the recordings of their favorite artists without having some numbers duplicated.

†Also released under the title of *Satchmo in Boston*.

concert. The other, *Satchmo at Pasadena,* on a single LP, contains only part of the program.

Although recorded on November 30, 1947, in Boston, *Satchmo at Symphony Hall* was not released until four years later. These two records, of course, give a pretty good idea of the type of concerts Louis and his band were giving at the time, though it is not one of the very best. Louis is well featured in *Muskrat Ramble, Black and Blue, Royal Garden Blues* (his best version of this famous number), *Mahogany Hall Stomp, On the Sunny Side of the Street,* and in a vocal duet with Velma Middleton on *That's My Desire* which is not quite as outstanding as the version from the Nice festival. Of course, Louis can be heard to some extent in other specialty numbers, except in Sidney Catlett's masterful drum solos on *Steak Face* and *Mop Mop,* which is the real title for *Boff Boff;* Velma Middleton never sounded better than on *Since I Fell for You;* Barney Bigard and the rhythm section are great in *C Jam Blues* and *Tea For Two,* just to mention the best of these specialties. One of the major interests of the two LPs is that they are the only ones which give us a chance to hear Sidney Catlett at great length and quite well recorded.

Satchmo at Pasadena, recorded January 30, 1951, at the Pasadena Civic Auditorium, California, is musically speaking superior to the Symphony Hall concert. Louis is featured more, for the specialities by other musicians have been reduced to three: *Honeysuckle Rose* by Earl Hines (a great performance), *Just You* by Barney Bigard, and *Star Dust* by Jack Teagarden. Besides, the fact that Earl Hines is on piano (instead of Dick Cary in the Symphony Hall LP) brings the solo work to a higher level. However, the Pasadena concert is not as well recorded as the Boston one. The rhythm section is too much in the background, only Arvell Shaw's bass can be adequately heard; and Cozy Cole's drums are much under-recorded. Even Louis' trumpet loses its fullness at times, but fortunately it is not affected by the slightest distortion.

In any event, *Satchmo at Pasadena* gives the atmosphere of Louis' concerts better than those at Symphony Hall. The duet with Velma Middleton, *Baby It's Cold Outside*, testifies more than any other recording to the sparkling verve and humor that Louis usually showed when singing with Velma. One can feel that the audience when not bursting with laughter is waiting with bated breath for the next word to come.* Velma also sings and dances during *The Huckle Buck,* and when she dances between her two vocals the band swings plentifully and Louis improvises two trumpet choruses that are out of this world.

Satchmo at Pasadena also offers an example of the amazing way Louis has of announcing the title of the number he is going to play. Just listen to him pronouncing *"Way Down Yonder in New Orleans"* and you'll notice that by the way he says those words he is setting the tempo in which he wants the number to be played. In fact, Earl Hines on the piano begins exactly in the tempo given by Louis' announcement. As far as Louis' trumpet part is concerned, *Way Down Yonder in New Orleans* is one of the most attractive interpretations of this concert.

It should be mentioned that one of the numbers recorded at this concert, *Big Daddy Blues,* sung and danced by Velma Middleton and released as a single, has never

---

*The 45 and 78 issues of *Baby, It's Cold Outside* have been considerably shortened.

been included in the various editions of *Satchmo at Pasadena*.

In the meantime, the Decca Company kept on recording Louis in short interpretations for release as singles with very different pick-up groups: sometimes a choir and a rhythm section *(Sit Down You're Rockin' the Boat, That's What the Man Said)*; the Gordon Jenkins Orchestra with violins *(When It's Sleepy Time Down South, Indian Love Call, Chloe*, etc.); small studio groups *(A Kiss to Build a Dream On, I Get Ideas, Because of You, Cold Cold Heart, I Laughed at Love)*. The latter ones are the best, especially *I Get Ideas* (the old tango *Adios Muchachos*), which Louis turned into a swinging piece, and *A Kiss to Build a Dream On*, in which the recording of Louis' voice is something to be marveled at. This number was to become a permanent feature of his stage set. In *Because of You*, for the first time, Louis is heard playing trumpet accompaniment to his own vocal chorus by the process of re-recording (double tracking).

In some recordings of this period Louis is surrounded by his own All Stars *(I'll Walk Alone* and *Kiss of Fire)*, most of the time augmented by a saxophone section and a guitarist (*Your Cheating Heart, Ramona*, and *April in Portugal*, three wonderful interpretations), or by many more musicians *(Sittin' in the Sun* and *Dummy Song)*.

Also to be mentioned is a good recording session in October, 1953, with a big band, The Commanders, which resulted in a new version of Louis' composition, *Someday You'll Be Sorry*, which is very different from the original; *I Can't Afford to Miss This Dream*, and best of all, a magnificent rendition of *The Gypsy*. Another session with an orchestra and choir, directed by Gordon Jenkins, saw the recording of *Bye and Bye, Trees, Spooks*, and *The Whiffenpoof Song*, a satire about the boppers.

The Music of Louis Armstrong on Records   127

Beginning in 1954, and for about the next eight years, Louis Armstrong made long-playing records almost exclusively and some of his greatest interpretations were recorded during this period.

First, Decca released a very pleasing ten-inch LP under the title of *The Glen Miller Story,* because two of the numbers had been performed in a film of the same title, *Otchi-tchor-ni-ya (Dark Eyes)* and a new version of *Basin Street Blues. Margie,* featuring Trummy Young (trombone and vocal), and a new version of *Struttin' With Some Barbecue,* recorded in 1954 with the All Stars, were included on this LP.

From now on, Louis, no longer an exclusive artist, recorded alternately for different labels. In 1954 the Columbia Company had Louis and his All Stars cut an LP which made a tremendous impression on the jazz world, *Louis Armstrong Plays W. C. Handy,* all the numbers being Handy's compositions: *St. Louis Blues, Beale Street Blues, Memphis Blues, Aunt Hagar's Blues, Hesitating Blues, Ole Miss, Loveless Love, Long Gone, Atlanta Blues, Chantez-les Bas,* and *Yellow Dog Blues.*

This is one of the most beautiful series of recordings made by Louis since the Hot Five days. But for one musician (Barrett Deems, drums) the band was ideal. In Barney Bigard, one of the greatest New Orleans clarinetists, and in Trummy Young on trombone, Louis had two perfect partners in the front line. Billy Kyle on piano and Arvell Shaw on base partly compensate in the rhythm section for the meager swing of Barrett Deems.

The band outdid itself in these recordings of Handy's numbers. There is a good reason for it: the musicians were entirely free to play as they wished without any type of restrictions, including the length of time that they played. *St. Louis Blues* lasts about nine minutes, most of the other numbers averaging five minutes. Thus, Louis and his musicians were able to improvise as much as they wanted, taking extra choruses whenever they felt like it. After three recording sessions, July 12, 13, and 14, 1954, the musicians were unanimous in saying: "It's no work, it's a pleasure to record under such conditions."

The listener can feel it; the band plays every number of the LP with fire and enthusiasm seldom heard in recording studios. On trumpet, Louis states or paraphrases the themes to perfection, improvises stupendous solos and reaches a climax in most of the collective improvisations at the end of the numbers, sometimes repeating a few powerful notes during the entire last chorus, a process which suits the blues perfectly *(Aunt Hagar's Blues* and *St. Louis Blues)*. But it is in *Chantez-las Bas* that the most unbelievable last chorus is to be heard. All the way through Louis just plays a prolonged glissando, ending in a very high register which engenders tremendous swing.

Next to Louis, it is Trummy Young who contributed most to the exceptional level of this LP. The listener can scarcely fail to realize that Trummy is one of the greatest and most powerful trombones jazz has ever known. Inspired by Louis, he returns the given stimulation. During the last chorus of *Loveless Love, Chantez-les Bas, Ole Miss,* and *Atlanta Blues,* Trummy's trombone impetuously pushes the whole band and obviously stimulates Louis to swing overwhelmingly. The trombone solo of *Chantez-les Bas* is among the best that Trummy ever recorded.

On the whole, the *Louis Armstrong Plays Handy* LP has benefited from good recording, especially Louis' voice and the trombone part. However, Louis' trumpet was captured better on other occasions. The fullness and amplitude of Louis' tone are not entirely present. Only *Aunt*

Hagar's Blues comes near to his real sound, especially at the beginning when Louis states the three successive themes of the number.

Anyway, the *Louis Armstrong Plays Handy* LP had the happy result of enlightening all the people whose good faith had been shattered by the tedious criticism directed against Louis for several years ("Armstrong lost his power"—"He's unable to play as he used to," etc.). Confronted with this abundant and splendid trumpet part and a masterful use of the high register, one could only conclude that Louis had not lost a bit of his exceptional talent. He still had his "iron" lips and was still blessed with the incredible inventiveness that had left his mark on the whole of jazz music. Some sad souls whispered that "Armstrong was playing too much like Armstrong." Others went so far as to say, "It is not Armstrong who is playing in this record; he wouldn't be able to do this; it is another trumpet player." This reminds me of the man who listened to a broadcast featuring a virtuoso and said, "I know of nobody able to play that much; it is certainly a record that they are playing over the air."

The success of *Louis Armstrong Plays Handy* caused Columbia to record another LP of the same kind the following year. It was *Satch Plays Fats*, in April–May 1955, in which Louis and his All Stars—the same musicians as before—played Fats Waller tunes: *I've Got a Feeling I'm Falling, Black and Blue, Honeysuckle Rose, Ain't Misbehavin', I'm Crazy About My Baby, Blue Turning Grey Over You, All That Meat and No Potatoes, Keepin' Out of Mischief Now,* and *Squeeze Me.* The music is almost equal to that of the *Handy* LP but the recording is a little less good, for the drums are over-recorded and the trumpet at times has a kind of nasal sound which never existed in Louis' tone. *All That Meat and No Potatoes,*

Ain't Misbehavin', and *Blue Turning Grey Over You* are for me the three best interpretations of the LP. Here, for the first time, *Ain't Misbehavin'* was recorded as Louis used to play it in such places as the Apollo Theatre in Harlem, with a lengthy coda during which he was ad-libbing on trumpet supported only by drums and hand-clapping of the chorus girls and members of the band, even some of the audience. It is a pity that the drummer for this recording was Barrett Deems; a Cozy Cole or a Sidney Catlett was really needed. It is also a pity that the tape of *Blue Turning Grey Over You* has been edited in such a way that there are two perceptible changes of tempo during the last chorus: obviously eight bars of another take of *Blue Turning Grey Over You* made on the same day have been squeezed in.

In the meantime the Decca Company recorded Louis while playing in a Los Angeles night club January 21, 1955, and issued two LPs entitled *Louis Armstrong at the Crescendo,* a beautiful double-album superior to the previous live LPs (Symphony Hall and Pasadena) for two reasons. One, the recording is better and more lively; second, with a few exceptions jazz musicians are more relaxed when playing in a nightclub than on stage, which is very noticeable here. It is to be added that Louis was in exceptional form that night, happy and full of pep, which one can feel even by the way in which he announces the numbers. *Louis Armstrong at the Crescendo* is a precious document from all points of view. It is the best of all Louis' live recordings and it is the one which gives the most accurate idea, in terms of program and atmosphere, of Louis when heard in person. His trumpet is wonderfully recorded with his real tone, his own color, his warmth and big volume, especially in *When It's Sleepy Time Down South, Jeepers Creepers, Tin Roof Blues, Lazy*

River, The Whiffenpoof Song, * and *When You're Smiling.*
His voice is just as well recorded as his trumpet (the vocal
duet with Trummy Young on *Rocking Chair* is the best
of the numerous recordings of this number by Louis). Of
course, there are a few passages of lesser interest which
are not found in the *Handy* or *Fats* LPs (specialities by
some musicians, such as the drum solo on *Mop Mop* and
the overlong clarinet coda in *Rose Room,* etc.) but on the
whole, what an album!

During Louis' European tour in 1955, with Edmond
Hall in place of Barney Bigard on clarinet, Columbia recorded several concerts, and the following year released
an LP entitled *Ambassador Satch,* Louis being considered an ambassador of the United States owing to the
beauty and success of his music. Despite the applause,
shouts, or laughs of the audience heard in all the numbers,
only three were actually recorded live in Amsterdam,
October 29, and they probably are the best: *Muskrat
Ramble, Tin Roof Blues,* and *Undecided.*† All the other
numbers were studio recordings: *West End Blues, The
Faithful Hussar, Dardanella,* and *Tiger Rag* in Milan,
December 20, 1955, and *All of Me* and *Twelfth Street Rag*
in California, January 29, 1956. The applause and other
noises were added later. The funny thing is that these
artificial noises are more distracting to the listener than
those on the live recordings; there are somewhat too
many of them, and they do not always come on with the
come on—at the right time, that is. If anyone is in need
of proof of this trick, in *Muskrat Ramble* (recorded live)

*This number has unfortunately been withdrawn in several editions
of *Louis Armstrong at the Crescendo* in both France and England.
Why?

†A fourth, *When It's Sleepy Time Down South,* was released later on
another LP.

the string bass ceases to be heard a little before and after Arvell Shaw's solo; this is during the time that Arvell goes out to the central mike and then back to his place at the end. Nothing of the kind happens in *Royal Garden Blues* and *The Faithful Hussar*, where there is not the least interruption in the bass playing before or after the solo.*

Around the same time, Columbia and Decca were recording some singles aimed at the juke-box industry. Columbia was the winning competitor with *Mack the Knife* in September, 1955, the old song from the *Three Penny Opera* in which Louis sang with amazing swing and which was one of his best sellers. Decca gave Louis the opportunity to record some good interpretations with his All Stars, augmented by a few other musicians: *Sincerely, Only You, Moments to Remember, Christmas in Harlem,* and *Christmas in New Orleans* (1955); some duets with Gary Crosby were less successful.

In 1956, the Columbia Company recorded Louis live three more times, at the Newport Festival, in Chicago, and in New York. With the exception of *Whispering,* Columbia released only numbers which Louis had recorded several times before (and recorded better). One of the Columbia spokesmen complained that Louis did not want to play new numbers during these concerts. But the truth is that the man responsible for the choice of the numbers to be released did not appreciate a part of Louis' repertoire, and thus we never got on record the wonderful duet with Velma Middleton, *Ko Ko Mo,* which Louis used to play at all the concerts of this period and on which he

---

*There are several other details proving that most interpretations on this LP have not been recorded live. I have given them all in the December, 1956, issue (No. 63) of the *Bulletin of the Hot Club de France* (65, Faubourg du Moustier, 82-Montauban, France).

invariably blew superb trumpet choruses. This stage version of *Ko Ko Mo* was ten times better than the one recorded by Decca where Louis duetted with Gary Crosby. However, it is not yet too late to despair of hearing this Louis-Velma version, and let us hope that Columbia will dig it out of their files, along with others, thus giving the public a chance to hear it.

In 1956, the Verve Company also began to record Louis, producing an LP of vocal duets with Ella Fitzgerald, *Ella and Louis*, accompanied by the Oscar Peterson Quartet, which included *Can't We Be Friends*, *Tenderly*, and nine other numbers. Better recorded than the old Ella-Louis duets (except when it comes to the trumpet solos), they are not as well accompanied, for Peterson's style did not fit too well with Louis'. Verve recorded Louis and Ella together again in 1957, still with Peterson, this time for an album of two LPs including twelve duets, some of them very successful *(Don't Be That Way, Stompin' at the Savoy)*, and four numbers interpreted by Louis alone (his *Makin' Whoopee* is especially fine) but, again, the tone of his trumpet lost some of its richness in the recording.

Louis and Ella were also reunited in a Verve album of *Porgy and Bess*, but Louis appears only in a few numbers.

There were three more Verve LPs recorded by Louis in 1957. One, accompanied by the Oscar Peterson Quartet, contains *Just One of Those Things, That Old Feeling*, and *Moon Song*, to mention only the best, but once more the Verve engineers were unable to catch the fullness and beauty of tone that Louis gets from his trumpet. The two other sessions were made with a big studio orchestra directed by Russell Garcia and sometimes including strings. Louis seems to have enjoyed playing in such an environment more than with Peterson. Whatever the reason, his trumpet solos (much better recorded) are generally of a higher inspiration, especially those on *Top Hat, White Tie and Tails, East of the Sun*, and *You're Blasé*. Although sung before a background of strings playing in a way that has little to do with jazz, *Nobody Knows the Trouble I've Seen* is perhaps the best of all the versions of this famous spiritual recorded by Louis. Not only does he sing it poignantly, but he also plays a trumpet solo of incredible expressive power.

Much superior to all the Verve LPs are the four that the Decca Company recorded during the same period and released in a box under the title of *Satchmo: A Musical Autobiography*. It is a kind of musical panorama of the Louis Armstrong of the years 1923–1934, retracing this fundamental segment of Louis' career by recording new versions of many numbers he had already recorded during those years. An effort was made to reconstruct the conditions under which the original versions were made, from those of King Oliver's Creole Jazz Band to those of Louis' big band of the early '30s, not forgetting the Clarence Williams Blue Five, the accompaniments to blues singers, and the Hot Five in between. Forty-two performances were recorded in December, 1956, and January, 1957, and six others previously recorded were incorporated into that imposing set, in which Louis Armstrong himself introduced each number.

What, in fact, really makes the value of these recordings so considerable is not their reconstruction but the opportunity of hearing Louis interpret again, in all freedom, and at the age of fifty-six, many of the numbers he had recorded when young. It is fortunate that the aim was to remake—rather than to adapt. The only disappointment is the evocation of King Oliver's band, where a second trumpet, Yank Lawson, was added to Louis' All Stars for *Dipper Mouth, Canal Street Blues,* and *Snag It.* In not one of these three numbers is the perfect balance, ensemble cohesion, and high spirit of King Oliver's Creole Jazz Band recaptured.

With the exception of the four blues sung by Velma Middleton (with an accompaniment of superb trumpet breaks, especially in *Reckless Blues* and *Court House Blues*), the other interpretations belong to two different categories: the one which roughly follows the routine of the Hot Five of 1925–1928, recorded by the regular Louis Armstrong All Stars (Trummy Young, Edmond Hall, Billy Kyle, Squire Girsch, and Barret Deems) plus an added guitar; the other includes those built up from the 1929–1934 recordings with a big band. For the latter, which constitutes practically the whole of the last two volumes, the All Stars and a guitarist are augmented by four very good saxophonists.

The series made up on the Hot Five formula is less successful than the original for an obvious reason. The exceptional quality of the Hot Five numbers and music, with its collective improvisations, was mostly due to Johnny Dodds and Kid Ory in the first Hot Five, and Earl Hines and Zutty in the second, all of whom were perfect partners for Louis Armstrong, expressing themselves exactly in the same musical spirit. The collective improvisations of this *Autobiography* do not have the same cohesion. Only Trummy Young plays in a style which blends perfectly with that of Louis Armstrong. As for Edmond Hall, he has little feeling for ensemble playing and his clarinet part is often in Louis' way. Then there is the fact that Louis' trumpet is generally not as well recorded in the first two volumes of the *Autobiography* as in the last two.

A little something is lacking in the last three sides of the *Autobiography* to make them fully satisfying; a better drummer than Barrett Deems is the missing factor. Louis Armstrong is featured a lot in those last three sides, both playing and singing in his most inspired way. It is fascinating to compare the new versions with the original ones. Although the routine (order of the choruses) is the same, Louis almost never plays his old choruses without giving them a different turn. He usually takes as a basis the variations he had improvised in the original versions, and what he creates could be described as variations on variations: *Some of These Days, I Can't Give You Anything But Love,* and *That's My Home* are striking examples of this. In other numbers, only a few details remind one of the original version; for instance, in *I Can't Believe That You're in Love With Me, Exactly Like You, King of the Zulus,* and *Georgia on My Mind.* One cannot, however, fail to notice that Louis has kept all the fresh inspiration of his youth and contrary to what some incompetent or ill-tempered critics have said, his inventiveness and instrumental mastery had not diminished one bit.

There does not seem to have been much tape-editing in the *Autobiography.* The only obvious instance is to be found in *On the Sunny Side of the Street,* where the two vocal choruses have been reduced to one by taking the first four bars of the first chorus and following them with the twenty-eight bars of the second, something easy to detect both by the difference in Louis' singing and the saxophone background.

However, the interpretations recorded before *Autobiography,* and which have been incorporated into it, have all but one been badly truncated in a shameful way. The one which has escaped editing is *When It's Sleepy Time*

Down South (the version from the *Crescendo* LP). In *Monday Date* (version from the *Pasadena* LP) four choruses have been taken out and among them the *trumpet solo!* In *Muskrat Ramble* (version from the Symphony Hall LP), the second trumpet solo has disappeared. In *Struttin' With Some Barbecue* (from the 1954 version of the *Glenn Miller Story* LP) the first half of the trumpet solo has been excluded (the second half of this solo immediately follows the first half of the second ensemble chorus). Several ensemble choruses have disappeared from *Basin Street Blues* (from the same *Glenn Miller Story* LP) and from *New Orleans Function* (1950). Such proceedings are inexcusable, the more so that during the 1960s it is these same truncated versions instead of complete ones which have been reissued in various Louis Armstrong LPs. As there is no logical reason for this, it is to be assumed that the person responsible for these Decca reissues forgot all about the original versions or was never aware of them.

While recording *Autobiography* for jazz-minded people, the Decca Company had Louis record interpretations aimed at the commercial market. They produced an LP called *Louis and the Angels* in which Louis was backed by a studio group with strings and a choir composed of four female and three male voices. The reason for the title of this LP is that it is composed entirely of numbers with the word *angel* or *heaven* in their titles: *And the Angels Sing, Angel Child, When Did You Leave Heaven, Angela Mia,* etc. The syrupy susurration of the choir and strings is supposed to create a celestial sound as possibly conceived by a Hollywood big businessman. The sleeve notes describe, with unconscious humor, the effect they were after:

As you enjoy listening to this album you might picture Louis as a cherub and the female choir as a heavenly harem of angels in high fly. . . . No matter what your eventual prospects for a more permanent association with such celestial company may be, you will commence to leave with the angels when you hear this music. . . . Fasten your seat belts . . . adjust your haloes . . . we're off on a musical jaunt with Louis and a band of angelic hosts.

Despite the saccharine background which has very little to do with jazz (save on the *Prisoner's Song,* which is well swung), Louis sings and plays as wonderfully as usual. He is one of the few jazz musicians capable of creating beautiful music in such an atmosphere!

A year later, in February, 1958, Decca had Louis record a complete LP of twelve spirituals entitled *Louis and the Good Book.* Here, too, there is a choir, ten voices whose singing is not really genuine, but Louis is helped well by his All Stars and the music swings much more than in the *Angels* LP. Louis revives these famous spirituals: *Down by the Riverside, Swing Low Sweet Chariot, Sometimes I Feel Like a Motherless Child, Go Down Moses,* and *Rock My Soul,* singing them in his own catching style like no one had sung them before. He also takes poignant trumpet solos in *Go Down Moses* and *Sometimes I feel Like a Motherless Child.* The *Good Book* had tremendous sales because it was welcomed by both real jazz fans and the general public. So far as I know, it was Louis' best-selling LP and probably still is.

The next two Armstrong LPs were produced by the Audio Fidelity company: *Satchmo Plays "King" Oliver,* 1959, and *Louis and the Dukes of Dixieland,* 1960.

The title of the first record should not be taken literally. King Oliver only recorded or composed four of the numbers to be found in the LP and there is no attempt to reproduce jazz as King Oliver used to play it. It does not really matter, for the music is great. Louis heads his regular All Stars and his trumpet is marvelously recorded, never better, in fact. *St. James Infirmary, I Ain't Got Nobody, Jelly Roll Blues,* and *Old Kentucky Home* are the best interpretations of an album on which the only thing to be regretted is the inclusion of too many short performances. It is difficult to understand why numbers like *Doctor Jazz* and *Drop That Sack* have been limited to two and a half minutes and two and three-quarter minutes respectively, which is shorter than the average length of the old 78 records. If the replacement of Barrett Deems on drums by Danny Barcelona slightly improved the rhythm section of the All Stars, Peanuts Hucko on clarinet is no better as an ensemble player than Edmond Hall.

The Dukes of Dixieland who surrounded Louis in the other Audio Fidelity LP are white musicians attempting to play in the New Orleans style. At first one would probably imagine this record to be much inferior to the *Plays Oliver* LP, but this is not the case. Here, all the interpretations take advantage of long-playing conditions and, what is more important, we have in nine of the twelve numbers an abundant ration of Louis' trumpet. He plays no less than four choruses (a hundred and twenty-eight bars) in *Avalon,* and five choruses (a hundred and sixty bars) in *Limehouse Blues.* The trumpet is perfectly recorded as in the *Plays Oliver* LP and Louis being in top form gives this record a value which many jazz fans did not everywhere realize, as they thought the Dukes of Dixieland were not going to be good enough to play with Louis. Despite their deficiencies, they are more appropriate partners for Louis than Oscar Peterson was and Louis sounds as though he was enjoying himself more playing with them than with some of the more or less progressive rhythm sections that were given to him at some recording sessions. Besides, this is the only opportunity on record to listen to Louis playing alternately with another trumpet player, Frank Assunto, who also benefits from the excellent recording. To hear them simultaneously and then in turn makes one realize the unique beauty of Louis' line and vibrato, the intensity of his swing, and the perfection of his phrasing. *Wolverine Blues, New Orleans, That's a-Plenty, Just a Closer Walk with Thee,* as well as *Limehouse Blues* and *Avalon,* make you sense Louis' genius.

In this same year, 1960, M-G-M recorded Louis with Bing Crosby under awkward conditions. This LP, called *Bing and Satchmo,* has Louis playing and singing with Bing Crosby and the Billy May Orchestra, sometimes with the addition of a choir. The orchestral background by Billy May was recorded *first.* This recording was then sent to Bing Crosby, who sang his part using earphones, which the M-G-M engineers mixed with the orchestral part. After that, it was all sent to Louis Armstrong and it was then his turn, also using earphones, to add his vocal and trumpet parts to the music already recorded. This procedure of recording the accompaniment first is a musical barbarism and it is especially harmful to a music like jazz in which creation and interpretation are often a whole. To force a soloist to improvise on an already recorded background (in other words, to accompany his own accompaniment) is not only reversing the natural procedure but it is also ignoring the important fact that in jazz there circulates an exchange of vibrations, of fluid elements, which act upon one another. However, Louis Armstrong does succeed in delivering some excellent choruses *(Preacher, Sugar, At the Jazz Band Ball).*

On April 3–4, 1961 the Roulette company showed intelligent initiative; they recorded together, for the first time, the two greatest musicians in jazz history—Louis Armstrong and Duke Ellington—*the* greatest soloist and *the* greatest band leader, and had them perform seventeen numbers. For years jazz enthusiasts had been wishing for these two giants to be recorded together;* they realized that it would be wonderful to hear Louis with Duke's band. It was, in actual fact, the reverse combination which took place, Duke being recorded with Louis' All Stars, taking the place of Billy Kyle at the piano. Duke's most original piano playing, added to the fact that all the recorded numbers were his own compositions, gave a strong "Ellingtonian" flavor to the music. Everyone recognized that contrary to what some people had predicted, the musical personality of Louis Armstrong, far from conflicting with Duke's, blended in perfect harmony. How could it be otherwise? Louis is the living incarnation of jazz and Duke almost all the time has had in his band trumpet players whose style was mainly influenced by Louis Armstrong: Cootie Williams, Freddie Jenkins, Rex Stewart, Ray Nance, Taft Jordan, and Cat Anderson, to name but a few.

During those two sessions Louis never tried to sound "Ellingtonian." For instance, he did not use a wa-wa mute in *Black and Tan Fantasy* or *The Mooche*. He merely had to play in his usual style to make his solos sound perfectly in accord with the atmosphere of these two numbers, and his admirable first chorus of *Mood Indigo* seemed tailormade for Duke's music. It is also easy to notice how Louis' singing and Duke's piano accompaniment fit together

---

*In *Long Long Journey,* the only side previously made with Louis and Duke (in 1945), Leonard Feather did not know how to turn this brief meeting to advantage (see page 119).

perfectly in *I'm Just a Lucky So and So.* All the interpretations recorded during those two sessions were successful, especially *It Don't Mean a Thing, Solitude, I Got It Bad* and, most of all, *The Beautiful American,* a blues in semi-fast tempo, orchestrated on the spot by Duke in the studio and in which Louis plays with electrifying power and swing.

Of course, the participation of Duke's ex-clarinetist Barney Bigard, who was now with Louis' All Stars, contributed to the cohesiveness of the interpretations—Barney being as familiar with Duke's music as with Louis'. Trummy Young on trombone was as outstanding as ever; Danny Barcelona and Mort Herbert were the other members of the All Stars for these two sessions (the timing of Mort Herbert's bass playing is the only thing which leaves something to be desired).

The last Louis LP for quite a while was to be *The Real Ambassadors,* recorded for Columbia in September, 1961. This strange record features such widely different musicians as Louis' All Stars, the Dave Brubeck Quartet, the vocal trio of Lambert-Hendricks-Ross and singer Carmen McRae. The numbers are extracts from a musical comedy composed by Dave and Iola Brubeck. The central aim of the record is to show that musicians like Louis Armstrong gain more friends for the United States than diplomats and the like. Hence the title.

While the musical themes are sometimes pleasant, the lyrics, which are often on the pedantic side, are unintentionally comical at times. At one point Louis has to sing, "In my humble way I'm the U.S.A. Though I represent the government, the government don't represent some policies I'm for. We learned to be concerned about the constitutionality in our nation—segregation isn't a legality" and other lyrics of the same type. So much so that when Dave

Brubeck, during the recording, asked Louis if he would like to stop for a while to "rest his lips," Louis replied, "It ain't my chops; they're all right. It's them words. . . . Don't worry about my chops."

Louis Armstrong and Trummy Young are the real stars of the record—all the best parts coming from them. Louis' main features are *Summer Song,* which he does by himself, *Cultural Exchange, Remember Who You Are,* and *King for a Day,* which he splits with Trummy Young.

Toward the beginning of the '60s there was a crisis in the record market. The expensive twelve-inch LP was not selling as well as in the 1950s. The buying public preferred 45s which were also better suited to the juke-boxes, being of shorter musical duration. They caused the recording companies to reduce their LP production, at least in the domain of pop music (jazz often being classified in this category), and they tried to obtain big sales through hit 45s.

That is why, in December, 1963, the Kapp Company recorded *Hello, Dolly!* and *A Lot of Livin' to Do* by Louis and his All Stars with the addition of a banjo.* *Hello, Dolly!* was an immediate success and such a great hit that the sales largely exceeded those of Louis' previous best sellers like *Blueberry Hill, C'est Si Bon,* and *Mack the Knife;* it even outsold the Beatles' best sellers of that time and those of any other pop group. The record world was both flabbergasted and bewildered: "So it is possible to get the biggest sales with high caliber jazz artists."

For it really was high-class jazz throughout the record. Louis is to be heard from the beginning to the end and the very pulse of jazz has never been more evident than in his

---

*A string background was later added but so distantly that several critics did not even notice it.

vocal choruses. His two trumpet choruses (one on each side) sound completely different from anything that he had played before. Often, Louis attacks notes at the very last moment, and for anyone feeling exactly what swing really is, the impression is phenomenal. By playing this way, any other musician would make the band drag the tempo. With Louis it is the complete opposite. As soon as he has attacked a note or phrase at the last moment, he gives it such an impulsion, makes the tempo live with such intensity, that he sets his whole band strongly into that tempo. You can feel the effect of his playing on the All Stars. Danny Barcelona and Joe Darensbourg (Louis' new clarinetist) never played better. Trummy surpasses himself; his phrases complement and continue Louis' phrases as perfectly as if their musical hearts beat exactly together. These are two of the most beautiful collective improvisations ever recorded. It is hard to put into words how beautiful these two choruses are. Louis' trumpet accent puts one under a spell. He starts each chorus with beautiful low notes followed by beautiful phrases in a higher register. And how he develops the melodic line! *Perfection!*

That record was somehow Trummy's swan song so far as his association with Louis Armstrong was concerned; a few days after the recording date, Trummy Young left the All Stars.

Because of the success of *Hello, Dolly!* the Kapp Company had Louis record ten more numbers with the All Stars in order to put an LP together, including *Hello, Dolly!* (which up until then was sold only as a single). *It's Been a Long, Long Time, I Still Get Jealous,* and *Moon River* were the best interpretations of this series. Louis' vocal and instrumental choruses are in the same vein as those of *Hello, Dolly!* The recording balance is not so good (too much piano and a background of strings that is not very discreet in a couple of numbers). "Big Chief" Russell Moore, although a good trombone for ensemble playing, does not reach the exceptional heights that Trummy did.

In the months and years to come, several record companies were to record Louis on short singles, trying hard to get another hit like *Hello, Dolly!* It was very naive to think that by doing exactly the same kind of thing one would get a second *Hello, Dolly!* The interpretations were taken at the same tempo and a loudly recorded banjo was added each time. The songs were of the same type as *Hello, Dolly!* too. That is how, during 1964–1967, *So Long Dearie, Faith, Mame,* two versions of *Cabaret,* and a few other numbers were successfully recorded, but they in no way reached the sales volume or musical quality of *Hello, Dolly!* and *A Lot of Living to Do.* Afterwards, disappointed by the results, the record companies went back to the formula of strings and choir as a background for Louis. Such was the case for *What a Wonderful World* and *The Sunshine of Love,* beautifully sung but without a single trumpet note. Although Louis asked in the recording studio to play some trumpet, the supervisor would either reduce it to the minimum or completely avoid it, pretending that only vocal records would sell well.* This made little sense, for the unprecedented success of *Hello, Dolly!,* which featured a full instrumental chorus, had been proof enough that a good ration of trumpet certainly did not hamper the commercial success of a Louis Armstrong record (in *Hello, Dolly!* the proportion

*When they let Louis play some trumpet they even reduced its volume! In several comparatively recent records, Louis' vocal choruses have twice as much volume as his trumpet notes, although his voice is by no means big.

is three-fifths singing to two-fifths trumpet).

So, with the exception of one version of *Cabaret* (on ABC-Paramount), of two numbers interpreted by Louis in the film *A Man Called Adam* (with Sammy Davis, Jr., 1965), *Someday Sweetheart,* and *Back o' Town Blues,* in which Pops plays magnificently and is well recorded (this *Back o' Town Blues* may be the best version of all those recorded by Louis), and with the exception of a few numbers in which Louis should not have been playing trumpet as he had been recently ill and had not entirely recovered *(Tin Roof Blues, Northern Boulevard Blues, Canal Street Blues,* and a new version of *When the Saints Go Marchin' In),* we have never had on record a full thirty-two-bar chorus (or the equivalent) since 1964. It is even more regrettable, for Louis' short solos recorded during those years (1965–1968) are not only superb but they are completely different from anything in the past; the simultaneous presence of an expressive power plus a supreme relaxation give to his playing an accent beautifully serene and at the same time poignant, which put the listener in a state of musical ecstasy *(Short but Sweet, Me, Myself and I, When You Wish Upon a Star).* Similarly, the melodic line of Louis' solos is more concentrated, and his increasingly precise phrases are shaped in a way that leads, more than ever, to a swinging way of playing. The extraordinary half-chorus on *I Like This Kind of Party* is a striking example of this, as are his solos in *'Bout Time, Ten Feet Off the Ground,** and the first choruses of *Canal Street Blues.*

So, at the age of sixty-eight, Louis Armstrong still had his most devoted fans and fervent admirers bewildered

---

* *Ten Feet Off the Ground, 'Bout Time, When You Wish Upon a Star,* plus eight other numbers are to be found on the LP titled *Disney Songs the Satchmo Way,* recorded with the All Stars, a choir and strings, which is the latest Armstrong LP (1968) at the time of writing.

by his increasing mastery, power and serenity. And one was entitled to wonder whether Louis could ever go any further on such a triumphant road.

Readers who have followed me to the end of this book, be persuaded that all you have been reading is *very little* compared to Louis Armstrong's music. Listen to it and *know how;* that is, receive it like those of his race do. It is the blacks and Mezz Mezzrow, a white who chose to be a black—who helped me understand Louis Armstrong. If it had not been for them, never would I have been aware of his greatness, only of a slight part of it. If you do not believe that the blacks can give the world musicians as great as the whites, there is no use insisting: you are racially prejudiced. But if, like a real music lover, you are attracted to this one, standing out like a gem in the middle of a degenerate century, then believe me and listen to Louis Armstrong with an unprejudiced ear. One day you will fully realize the genius of one of the greatest and most genuine musicians in the whole history of music: Louis Armstrong.

20 April 1969

THE BEST OF LOUIS ARMSTRONG
LPs AVAILABLE

The Louis Armstrong Story, Four Volumes (1925-31)
   Columbia CL 851/52/53/54

V.S.O.P. (1931-32)   Epic 22019

A Rare Batch of Satch (1932-33)   RCA Victor LPM 2322

Louis Armstrong in the '30s and '40s   RCA Victor LSP 2971

Rare Items (1935-44)   Decca 79225

Louis Armstrong Jazz Classics (1939-40)   Decca 8284

Satchmo at Symphony Hall (1947)   Decca DXS 7195

Satchmo on Stage (1950)   Decca 8330

Satchmo at Pasadena (1951)   Decca 8041

Satchmo Serenades (1949-53)   Decca DL 8211

Louis Armstrong — Autobiography,
   Four record boxed-set album (1957)   Decca DX 155

The Good Book (1958)   Decca DL 8741

Hello, Dolly! (1963-64)   Kapp 3364

IMPORTANT RECORDS BY LOUIS ARMSTRONG
WHICH ARE AVAILABLE

New Orleans Jazz (1940)   Decca 8283

Louis Armstrong Plays W. C. Handy (1954)   Columbia CL 591

Louis Armstrong at the Crescendo Club (1955)
   Decca DL8168/69

Satch Plays Fats (1955)   Columbia CL 708

Louis Armstrong with the Dukes of Dixieland (1960)
   or *Louis and the Dukes of Dixieland*   Audio Fidelity 5924

Louis Armstrong All Stars (with Duke Ellington
   at the piano) (1961)   Pickwick 3033